# THE Drumset Musician

## By Rod Morgenstein and Rick Mattingly

To access audio visit:
www.halleonard.com/mylibrary

"Enter Code"
3963-1192-3106-9573

ISBN 978-1-5400-2409-1

**HAL•LEONARD®**

7777 W. BLUEMOUND RD. P.O. BOX 13819 MILWAUKEE, WI 53213

In Australia Contact:
**Hal Leonard Australia Pty. Ltd.**
4 Lentara Court
Cheltenham, Victoria, 3192 Australia
Email: ausadmin@halleonard.com.au

Visit Hal Leonard Online at
**www.halleonard.com**

# CONTENTS

# Introduction

Welcome to *The Drumset Musician*. The following pages contain hundreds of beats and fills that will enable you to develop the necessary coordination and technique to handle a wide variety of rock, pop, funk, blues, and country songs. These are not just exercises; the patterns in this book have been used on countless recordings spanning several decades and can be applied to actual songs.

In addition, *The Drumset Musician* goes beyond just teaching you isolated beats and fills. You'll also learn how to use them to create drum parts to songs. As an added bonus, audio tracks are available at halleonard.com/mylibrary that contain play-along tracks so that you can use what you are learning and get the feel of playing with an actual band. Each of the songs is presented twice—once with a drum part played by Rod, so you can hear how the drums fit in with the song. Then there's another version of the same song, but without drums, so you can try playing the same part Rod played or you can create your own drum arrangement.

The following pages contain some basic information to get you started. Look them over and then get behind the drums and start playing!

# Music Reading Fundamentals

Different types of notes are used in music notation to indicate how long the note should last. Each note has a corresponding rest, which is used to indicate silence. The chart below shows the most common notes and rests:

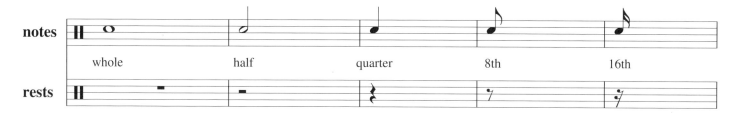

Each of the notes shown above is twice as long as the note following it. In other words, a whole note can be divided into two half notes; a half note can be divided into two quarter notes, and so on. The chart below shows the relationships between the note values. Notice how the "flags" that appeared on the 8th and 16th notes in the example above are connected into beams in the chart below.

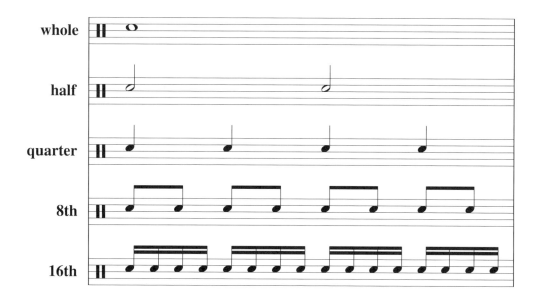

With most instruments, the sound of a half note lasts longer than the sound of a quarter note, the sound of a quarter is twice as long as that of an 8th note, and so on. But when you strike a drum, the sound is instantaneous and short, as though you were playing a 16th note. Nevertheless, longer note values are used in drum notation to indicate the amount of space between two notes as well as for clarity. By contrast, a cymbal crash will often be notated as a quarter or 8th note, even though the sound is supposed to ring over several beats.

Music is divided into measures by barlines, and each measure has a specific number of beats. At the beginning of a piece of music you will find a time signature. The top number tells you how many beats are in each measure; it can be practically any number, but it is most often between 2 and 12. The bottom number tells you what type of note receives one beat. If the bottom number is a 2, then a half note receives one beat; if the bottom number is 4, a quarter note gets one beat; if the bottom number is 8, an 8th note gets one beat, and so on.

For example, when the time signature is 4/4, there are four beats in each measure and a quarter note gets one beat. Therefore, each measure in 4/4 time must contain four quarter notes or something that equals four quarters, such as one whole note, two half notes, one half note and two quarters, eight 8th notes, or any combination of notes and rests that equals four quarters. (Chapters One and Two contain more specific information about counting rhythms in 4/4 time.)

If the time signature is 12/8, there are twelve beats in a measure and an 8th note gets one beat. Therefore, each measure in 12/8 time must contain twelve 8th notes or something that equals twelve 8th notes. (Chapter Three contains more specific information about counting rhythms in 12/8 time.)

## Using a Metronome

A big part of any drummer's job is to keep the tempo steady, which means you don't speed up or slow down while you're playing. A metronome is a device that can help you achieve this goal. It produces a steady click or beep, and it can be set to a variety of tempos. You can set the clicks to conform to whatever part of the pulse you wish. Most records are made with the use of a metronome or "click track."

Typically, the metronome is set to the quarter-note pulse of a song, and most of the charts in this book that go with the audio tracks have a marking at the top left in which you'll see a note followed by an equal sign and a number. This tells you where to set the metronome. With very slow tempos, the metronome marking might give you 8th notes, while with other tunes it might give you a dotted-quarter or a half note.

There are several different types of metronomes including wind-up, electric, and digital. There are also metronome apps for phones and tablets (many are free). You can use a drum machine as a metronome, in which case you can have sounds such as cowbell or shaker keeping the tempo.

Some people say that using a metronome will make your playing sound "stiff," but that's not true. Although it's not necessary to use a metronome every time you practice or play, the authors recommend that you use one frequently to help you get in the habit of keeping steady time.

# Other Symbols

Often, drummers play the same beat several times in a row. A repeat sign ∦ is used whenever you are supposed to repeat what you played in the previous measure. In the following example, you would play the beat in the first measure four times.

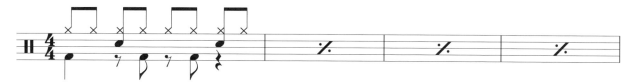

If two consecutive measures are to be repeated, you will see a two-bar repeat, as illustrated in the example below. This is only used when the two measures are different from each other, not when the same measure is to be repeated twice.

When an entire section of music is to be repeated, repeat dots are used. In the example below, you would repeat the music between the two sets of repeat dots.

If the repeat dots only occur at the end of a section of music, repeat all the way back to the beginning. In this book, most of the exercises have repeat dots at the end, indicating that you should play them over and over.

Repeated sections sometimes have 1st and 2nd endings. In the example below, you would play the first three measures, then repeat back to the beginning. Play the first two measures again, but this time skip measure three (the 1st ending) and play measure four (the 2nd ending).

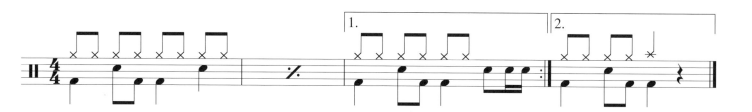

Drummers often have a certain amount of freedom in terms of what they play, so you will often see drum parts that have measures with "slash" notation, indicating that the drummer should be playing whatever is appropriate to the tune.

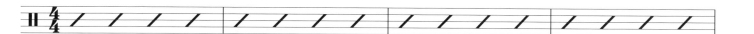

# Dynamics

The term "dynamics" has to do with how loudly or softly you are playing. Volume level is indicated with letters that represent Italian words for loud and soft. Some common dynamics are explained in the following chart:

| symbol | Italian term | meaning |
| --- | --- | --- |
| *ff* | fortissimo | very loud |
| *f* | forte | loud |
| *mf* | mezzo forte | medium loud |
| *mp* | mezzo piano | medium soft |
| *p* | piano | soft |
| *pp* | pianissimo | very soft |

If the music is supposed to gradually get louder, you might see the word crescendo or the abbreviation cresc. If the music is supposed to gradually get softer, you might see the word diminuendo or the abbreviation dim. You might also see the following symbols:

Crescendo: get louder ———◁      diminuendo: get softer ▷———

# Drumset Notation

Throughout this book, the drumset will be notated on a five-line music staff. At the beginning of each line of music you will see a clef. Different instruments use different clefs. Guitar music is written in treble clef; bass players use bass clef; keyboard players use a double staff that has both treble and bass clef. Although sometimes you will see drum music written in bass clef, it is more common to see it written in "rhythm" clef, indicating that the lines and spaces of the staff do not represent specific pitches.

treble 𝄞      bass 𝄢      rhythm ‖

The different parts of the drumset are assigned to the staff according to the following key:

bass drum   snare drum   small tom   medium tom   large tom   hi-hat   ride cymbal   crash cymbal

Various symbols are used to alter notes on occasion, as shown below:

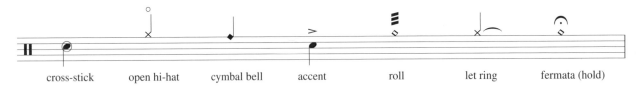

cross-stick   open hi-hat   cymbal bell   accent   roll   let ring   fermata (hold)

Sometimes you will see the snare drum part connected to the ride cymbal or hi-hat part, as in example a below. Other times, the snare drum part will be connected to the bass drum part, as in example b below. Both are played exactly the same way.

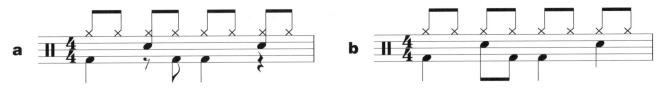

In this book, both methods of notation are used in order to expose students to each of them. In each case, the drumset is notated as two "voices" or lines: one with the note stems pointing up, the other with the stems pointing down. Each voice has to be complete within itself, so that is why you sometimes see rests in one voice, even though another element of the drumset is playing on that beat or count.

# Parts of the Drumset

The photo below shows a typical five-piece drumset with accompanying cymbals. Generally, the main beat is played using the snare drum and bass drum. The time feel is kept either on the hi-hat or ride cymbal. Crash cymbals are often used for accents while tom-toms can be used for fills and solos. But those are just general guidelines. Ultimately, any drum or cymbal can be used as part of the time feel or groove as well as for fills and solos.

Unlike most instruments, which are usually standardized (e.g., most guitars have six strings and are tuned the same way), a drumset can be customized to fit your personal style and the requirements of the music you play. Many good drummers use a minimum of equipment: bass drum, snare drum, one or two rack toms, one floor tom, one ride cymbal, one crash cymbal, and a pair of hi-hat cymbals. Other drummers might use two bass drums, four rack toms, two floor toms, and multiple ride, crash, and even hi-hat cymbals.

Keep in mind that having a bigger drumset does not make one a better drummer. The important thing is to use the right equipment for the style of music you play and for your personal drumming style. Even with the smallest drumset you can keep a strong groove and be rhythmically creative.

The exercises in this book can all be played on a five-piece drumset with hi-hat, ride, and crash cymbals.

# Playing Styles

Traditionally, drumset players have used their right hands to play the ride cymbal or hi-hat while the left hand played the snare drum. Some left-handed players do just the opposite. In a few cases (such as with Rod), the drummers reverse their setups so that the hi-hat is on the right and the bass drum is played with the left foot. These drummers still tend to "cross over" and play hi-hat with the left hand and snare drum with the right.

But some left-handed players use the same basic arrangement as right-handed players, except that the main ride cymbal is on the left. This allows them to play "open handed" with the left hand on the hi-hat and the right hand on the snare drum.

Looking at a standard setup, one might wonder why drummers traditionally play hi-hat with the right hand and snare drum with the left. To answer that question, one needs to take a quick look at drumset history. Early drumsets did not have hi-hat cymbals. They did have "sock" cymbals: two cymbals mounted on a pedal that were played with the left foot. But they were down by the floor and were only played with the pedal. When sock cymbals evolved into hi-hats, which allowed them to be played with a stick, drummers just reached over with their right hands and kept the left hand on the snare drum. Most of the playing was still done on the ride cymbal, so they were spending very little time with their hands crossed. Also, most drummers were using traditional grip, and it would have been awkward to reach up and play the hi-hat cymbals with the traditional left-hand grip.

As rock 'n' roll developed in the 1950s and '60s, drummers gradually began to play more hi-hat than ride cymbal. Many drummers also switched to matched grip, but they were so used to crossing over to play the hi-hat with the right hand that they continued doing it.

With the increasing influence of funk-based rock drumming, players started wanting the snare drum to be a lot louder than the hi-hat. This began to cause problems, as it was difficult to hit the snare drum very hard with the left hand when the right stick was in the way. (By contrast, in the '50s and '60s, snare drum and hi-hat were more equal in volume.)

In order to have more room to make a bigger stroke with the left hand on the snare drum, some drummers tried setting up the snare drum very low and the hi-hat very high. Drummers also started experimenting with auxiliary hi-hats that could be placed on the right-hand side of the drumset. Some consisted of a pair of hi-hat cymbals that were mounted in the closed position. A drummer could ride on this set of hats but use the regular set for pedal effects. Other auxiliary hi-hats featured cables that allowed the cymbals to be placed on the right-hand side of the setup and still have a pedal in the traditional position on the left.

Some drummers, though, began questioning the idea of crossing the hands. Today, some drummers play open-handed. When playing hi-hat and snare drum, they play the hi-hat with the left hand and the snare with the right. When playing ride cymbal and snare, they play the cymbal with the right and the snare with the left. Drummers who have spent years always playing both ride cymbal and hi-hat with the right hand and snare drum with the left might feel awkward the first time they try playing hi-hat with the left hand and snare drum with the right, but it doesn't take long to start feeling comfortable playing that way. Drummers who learn to play both ways from the very beginning never seem to have a problem switching back and forth, and they feel that their coordination is much better.

The authors encourage you to experiment with both open-handed and cross-handed playing. Neither one is more correct than the other; they are simply options. Ultimately, what matters is how you sound, and you should use the system that helps you sound the best.

## Protecting Your Ears

Drums are loud and the sound can eventually damage your hearing. Both of the authors of this book have a constant ringing in their ears (tinnitus) from years of playing drums without protecting their ears. Rod, of course, has played drums in large arenas with high-powered bands and huge sound systems. But you don't have to be playing in situations such as that to suffer hearing damage. Rick has mostly played in clubs in which the volume level was reasonably loud, although nothing like what Rod's bands were putting out. But he was practicing a lot in small rooms and teaching several hours a week in a small studio with unmuffled drums.

At first, after being exposed to loud music, most people will notice a ringing in the ears at night before they go to sleep. Usually the ringing will be gone the next morning. But that ringing is the first warning sign of ear damage. Eventually, the ringing will not go away, and it can get louder and louder to the point that you hear it all the time.

Drummers should always wear some type of hearing protection. Whether it's the foam earplugs you can buy at most drugstores, molded earplugs available from ear doctors and hearing specialists, or the type of headphones that are used at airports and on firing ranges, you must protect your hearing. (Vic Firth markets headphones that Rod helped design, and that are available at most music stores and drum shops.) When practicing in a small room, muffle the drums and cymbals or use a practice-pad setup.

You must begin protecting your ears before the damage occurs. You might very well play drums every day without wearing ear protection for twenty years or more without having your ears ring all the time, but once the ringing becomes constant, *it will never go away*.

# Chapter One
## 8th-note Beats

This chapter begins with rock beats featuring both 8th-note and quarter-note ride patterns. The examples in this section are all in 4/4 time, which is the most common time signature used in rock music. In fact, 4/4 is also known as "common time," and instead of the 4/4 time signature you will sometimes see a large C at the beginning of the staff.

We will start with an 8th-note ride pattern. In 4/4 time, 8th notes divide each beat in half, and so they are counted "1 & 2 & 3 & 4 &." To begin, play straight 8th notes over and over on the ride cymbal or closed hi-hat with one hand, counting as in the example at right.

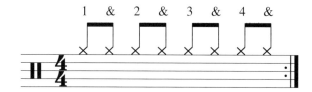

Next, play the ride pattern with one hand on the ride cymbal or hi-hat, and play the snare drum with the other hand on counts 2 and 4, as shown in pattern 1a on page 11. Then try playing the bass drum along with either the ride cymbal or hi-hat. The bass drum notes should be played on counts 1 and 3, as in pattern 1a on page 11. When you are comfortable with that, try playing ride cymbal (or hi-hat), snare drum, and bass drum together, as in pattern 1a on page 11.

On pages 11–20, the left column consists of patterns with an 8th-note ride. Although the notation shows the 8th notes on the hi-hat, the examples should also be practiced with ride cymbal. Use the 8th-note ride as a framework and keep it very steady. Practice slowly at first so you can concentrate on accuracy and precision. Once you are playing a pattern correctly, you can work on playing it at faster tempos.

The 8th-note ride pattern can be played two different ways. One way is to play all the notes evenly, at the same volume. But in many songs, drummers will accent the main beats (1, 2, 3, 4) and play the &'s softer, as shown in the example on the right. You should practice all the 8th-note patterns in this chapter both ways.

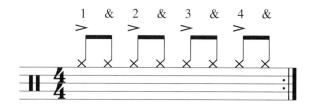

The right-hand columns on pages 11–20 feature beats with a quarter-note ride. In each example, the bass drum and snare drum are playing the same pattern as you go across the page. The only difference is in the ride pattern. Even though you will not be playing 8th notes on every beat, you should still count "1 & 2 & 3 & 4 &" throughout the pattern so that when you have an 8th on the second part of a beat in the bass drum or snare drum part, you will be able to place it precisely. Remember that the spaces between notes are just as important as the notes you play.

Listen to audio track 1 to hear how selected beats from this chapter should sound. Once you are comfortable with the patterns on a page, try playing them along with tracks 3, 5, 7, and 9.

## Left-foot Hi-Hat

When playing the ride cymbal, many drummers keep a pulse with the left foot on the hi-hat pedal. Two common hi-hat patterns are shown at right that can be used with the patterns in Chapter One. Be sure to bring the two hi-hat cymbals together sharply so as to produce a "chick" sound. Adding a fourth limb is a challenge, so be patient.

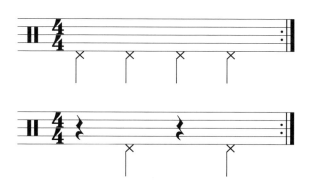

## Chapter One Recorded Examples

Audio track 1 features several examples from Chapter One to give you an overview of the types of patterns you will be learning. For convenience, each of the patterns played on track 1 is notated below.

Backbeat Pattern 3a (page 11)

Backbeat Pattern 20b (page 13)

Single Backbeat 1a (page 14)

Bass Drum Variation 3b (page 15)

Straight-four Snare Drum 3a (page 17)

Snare Drum Variation 2a (page 18)

Snare Drum Variation 12a (page 19)

Drumset Colors 6 (page 21)

Drumset Colors 7 (page 21)

Drumset Colors 9 (page 22)

Tom-tom Beat 7 (page 22)

4-beat Fill 11 (page 27)

# Backbeat Patterns

A lot of rock and pop drumming involves playing the snare drum on beats 2 and 4, which are commonly referred to as "backbeats." The first set of patterns will develop your ability to maintain consistent snare drum backbeats with a variety of bass drum variations.

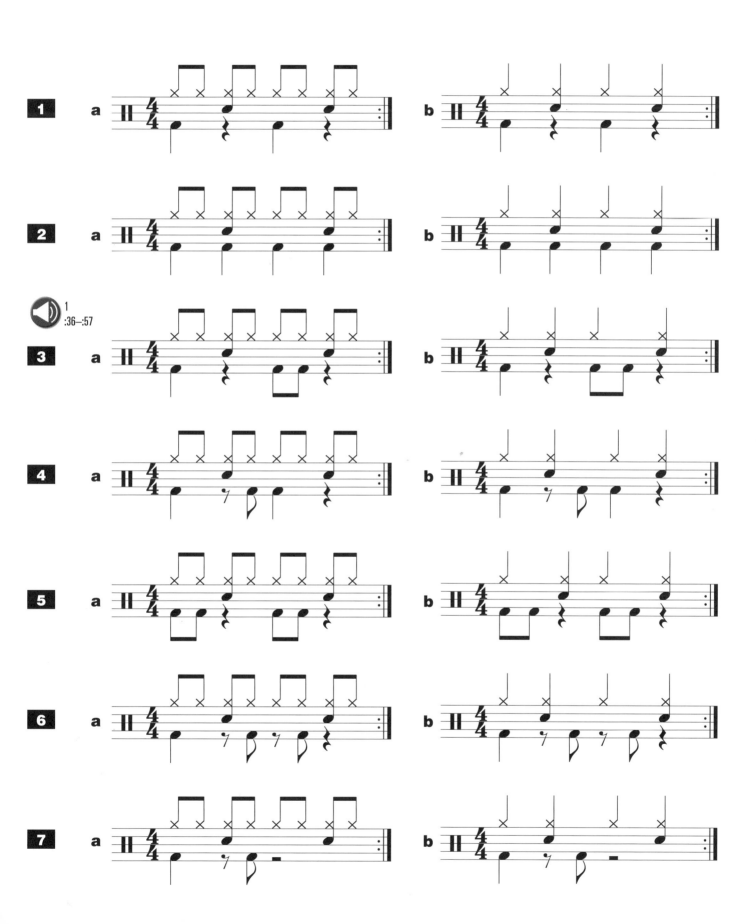

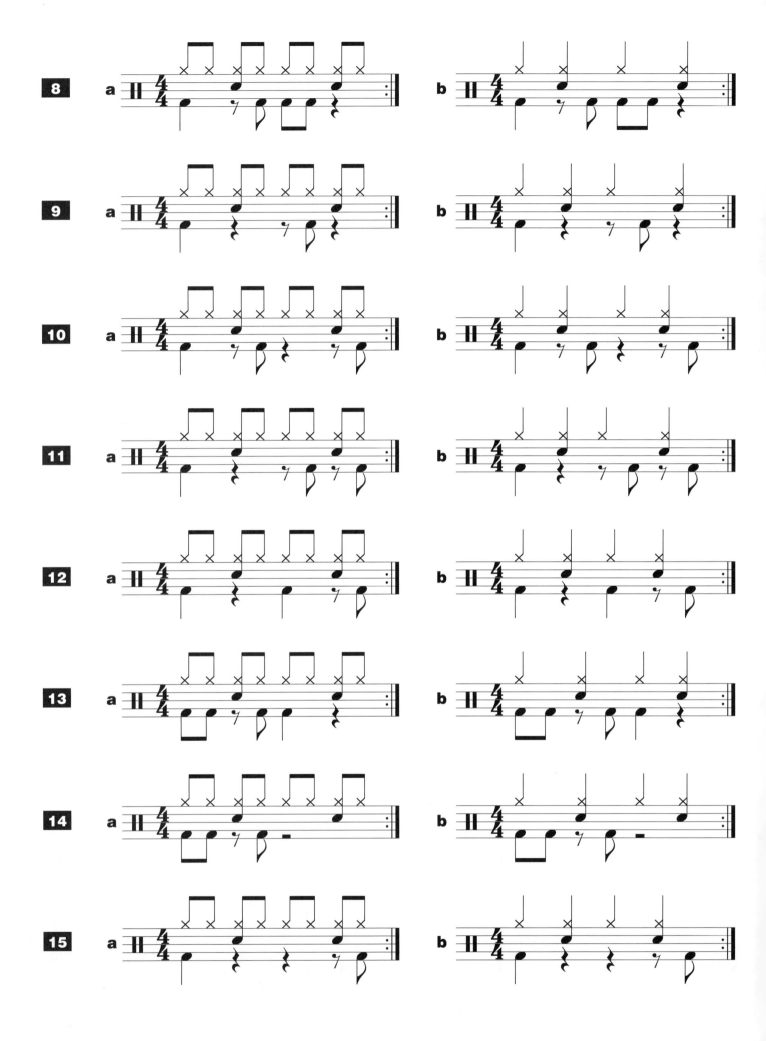

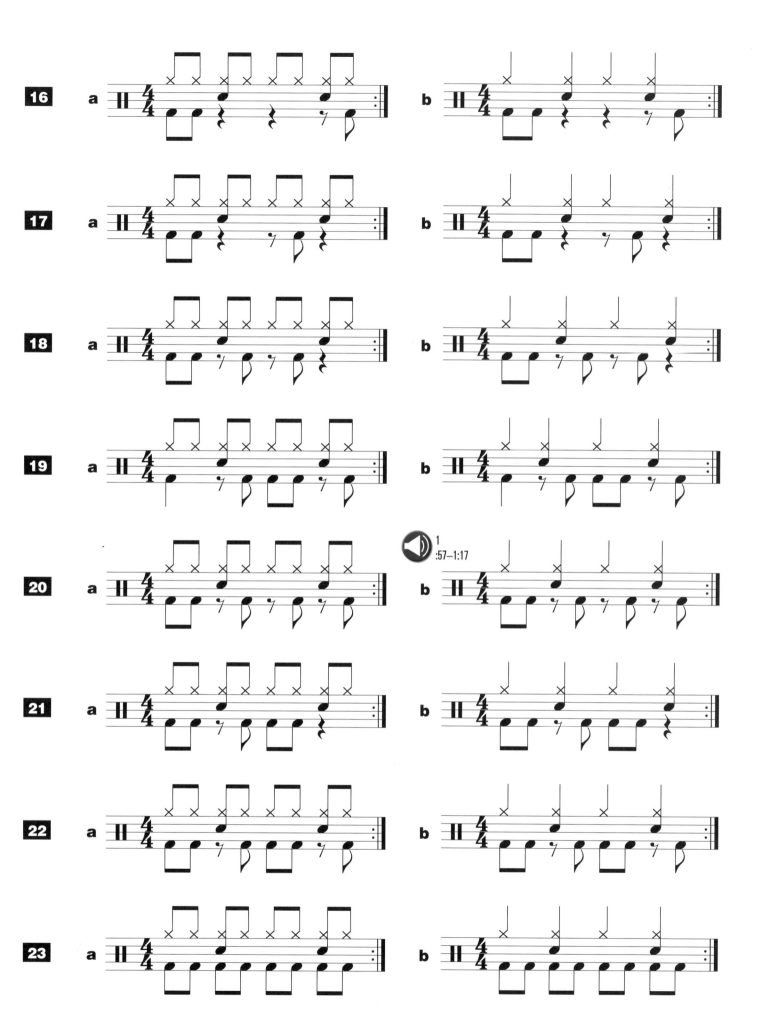

## Single Backbeats

Sometimes it is effective to play only one backbeat per bar instead of two, as in patterns 1 through 7. Playing a single snare note on beat 3, as in pattern 8, creates a half-time feel.

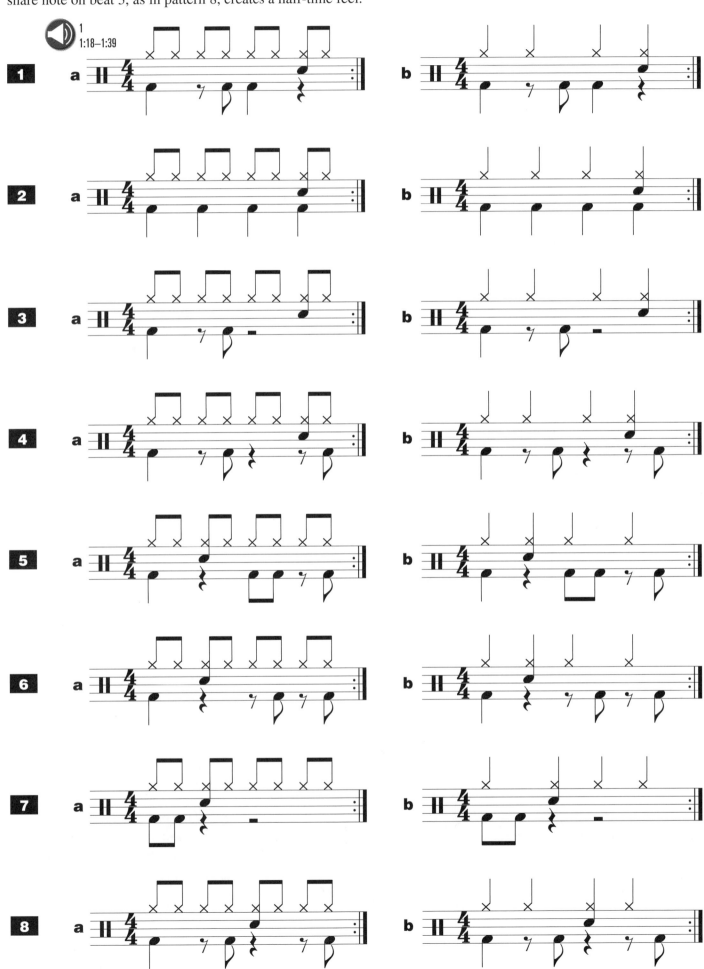

# Bass Drum Variations

Not always playing the bass drum on the first beat (downbeat) of the bar can give the music a different feel and make it less predictable. It is especially effective to leave out a bass drum downbeat on the second bar of a two-bar pattern. By keeping the snare drum on beats 2 and/or 4, as in the following examples, you can have more freedom to be creative with the bass drum without confusing the other musicians in the band or people who are dancing to your music.

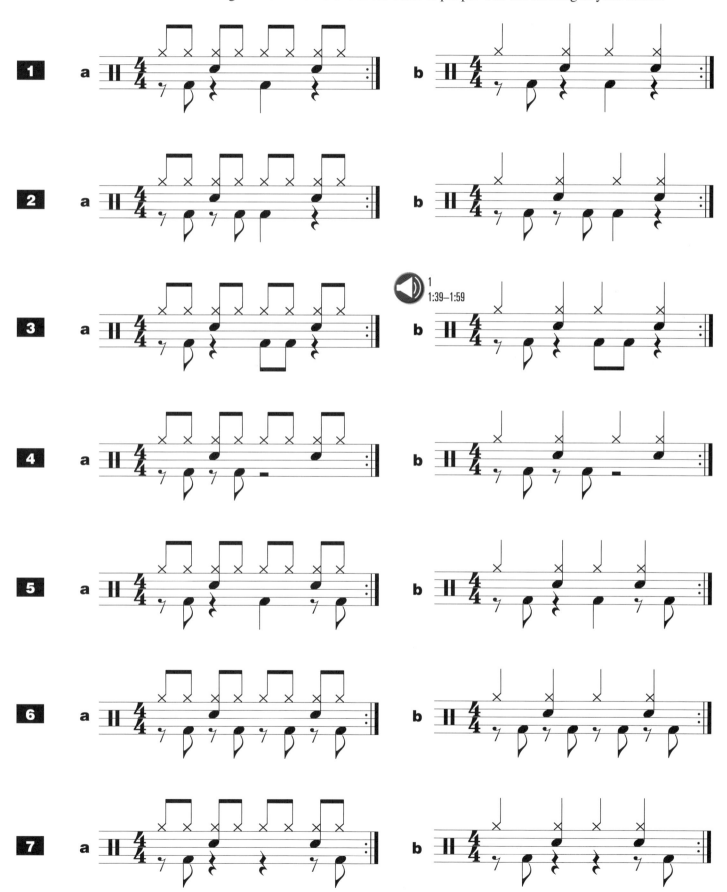

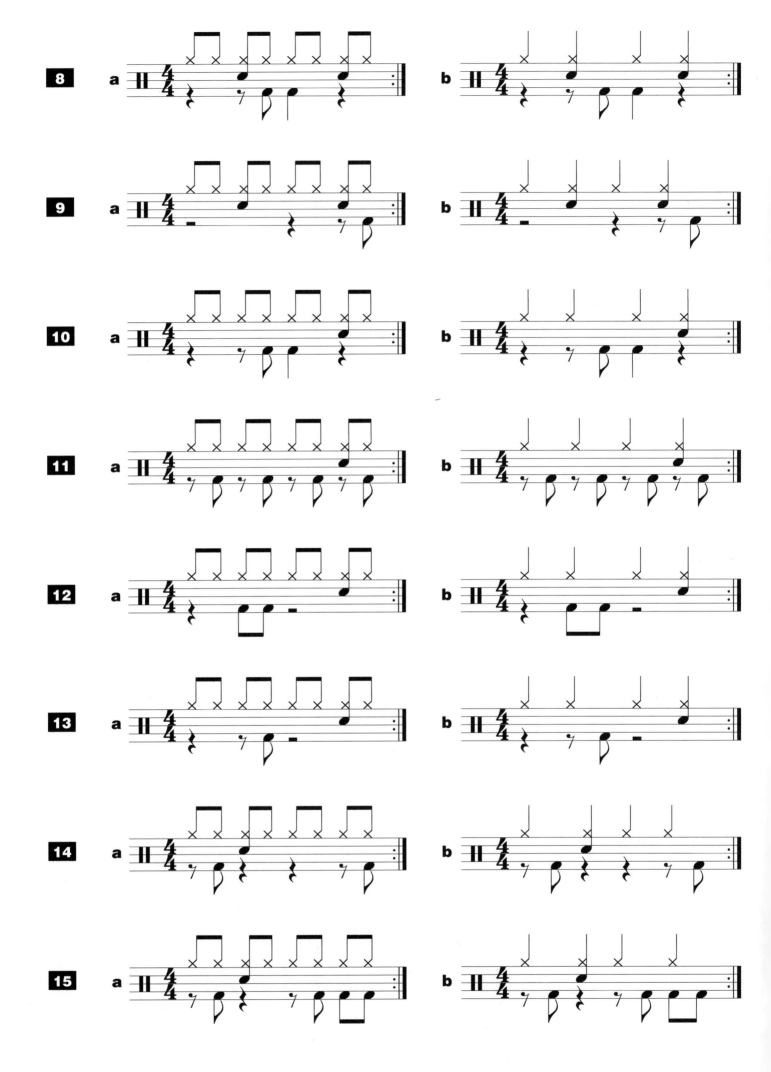

# Straight-four Snare Drum

Countless songs have been driven by beats featuring the snare drum playing on all four beats, as in the first six patterns below. Pattern 7 has a similar feel. It is common to spice up straight-four snare patterns with an occasional extra snare drum note, as in pattern 8.

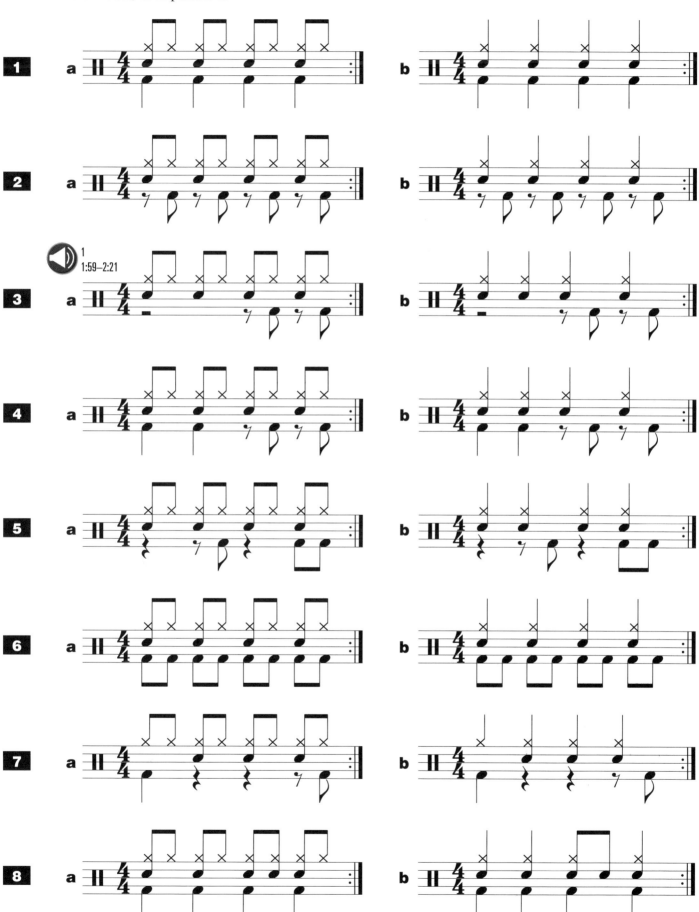

# Snare Drum Variations

As important as snare drum backbeats are in rock 'n' roll drumming, the snare drum can play other notes as well. One of the most popular snare drum variations used in the 1950s and '60s was the "double" backbeat on either the second or fourth beat, as illustrated in patterns 1 through 10. When practicing such beats, experiment with different accents and notice how they affect the feel. Apply each of the following variations to patterns 1 through 10.

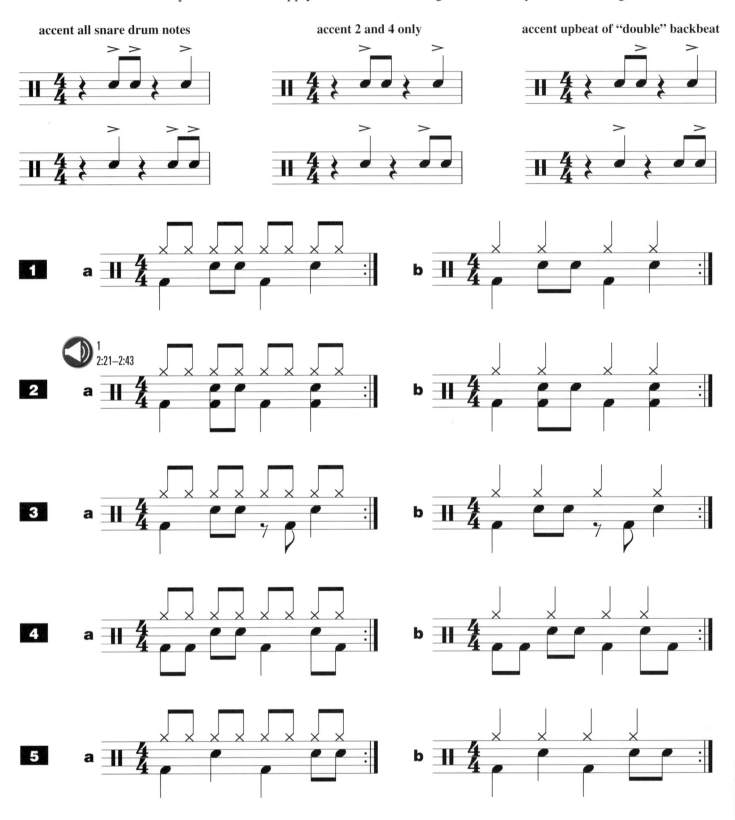

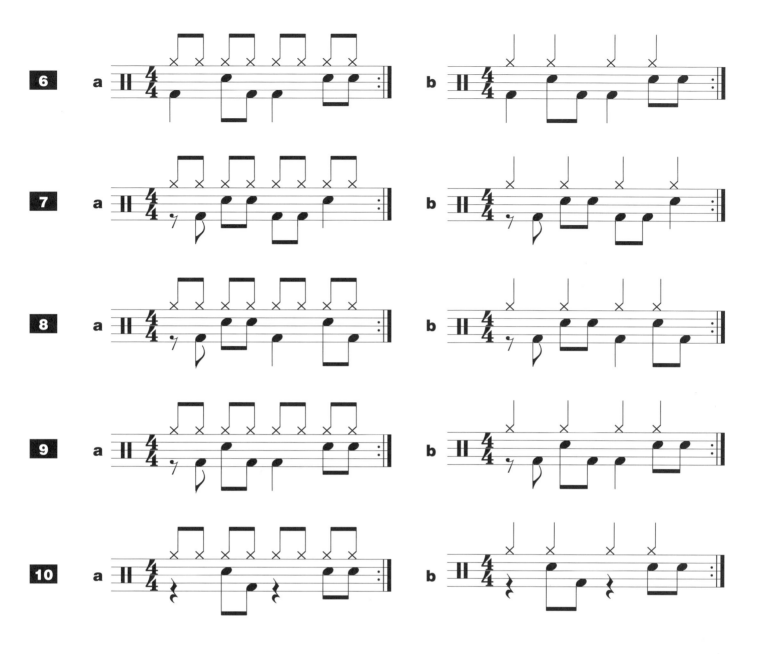

Playing backbeats "early" on the & of 1 or 3 (patterns 11, 12, and 13) or "late" on the & of 2 or 4 (patterns 14 and 15) is also effective in making the music less predictable, and playing such offbeat notes gives the music a "funkier" feel. Playing a strong snare drum on beat 3, as in patterns 16, 17, 18, and 19, creates a "half-time" feel. The final pattern features a New Orleans "second line" feel in the bass drum.

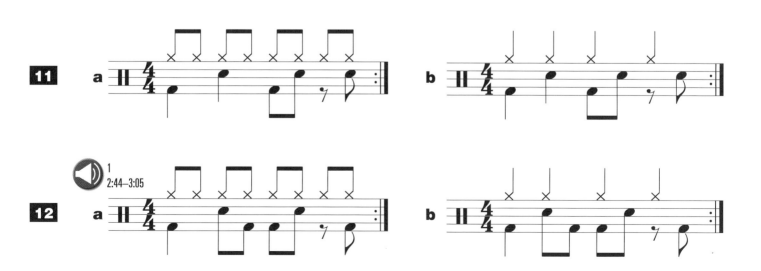

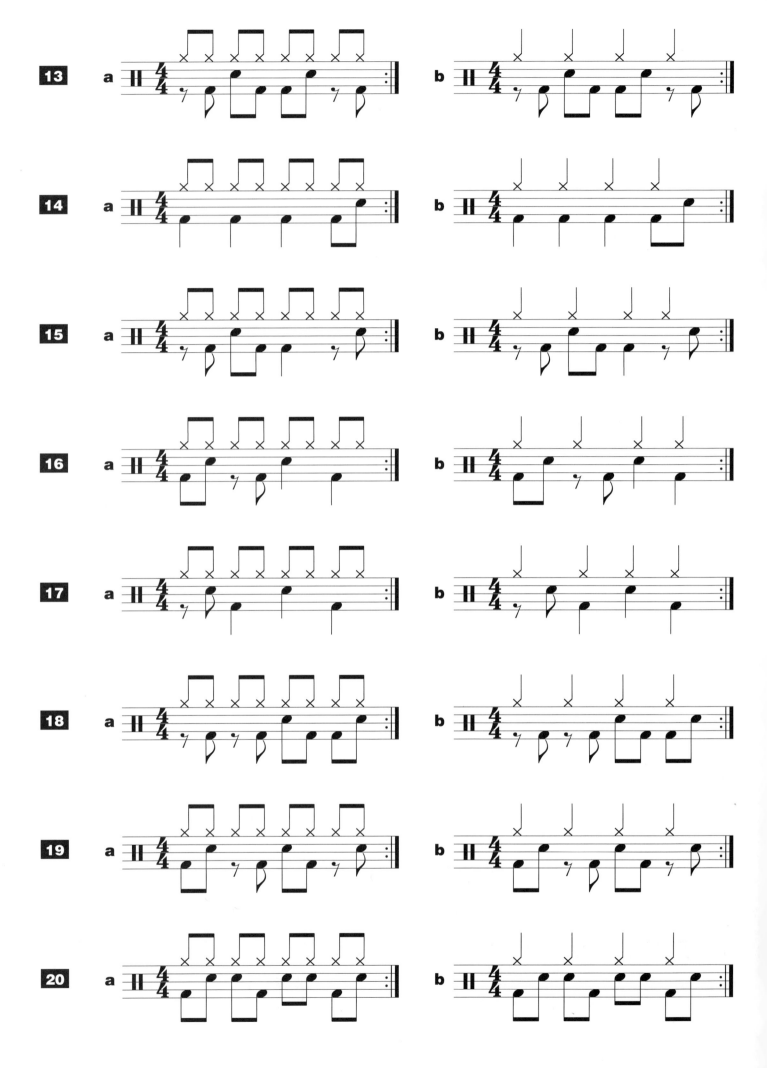

# Drumset Colors

Musicians often refer to different sounds and effects as "color." For example, when you change from hi-hat ride to cymbal ride, you are changing the color, even if you are still playing the same pattern. Experiment with a variety of colors on the drumkit. When riding on the hi-hat, you can keep the cymbals closed tightly or open them a little bit for a "sloshy" sound. You can ride on the body or the bell of the ride cymbal, on a crash cymbal, on a cowbell, on the rim of the snare drum or floor tom, or on the shell of the bass drum. Following are some other examples of drumset colors.

**Open Hi-Hat:** Opening the hi-hat on certain notes can add interest to a beat. Pattern 4 is a classic "disco" groove. Note: on Pattern 4, you will be closing the hi-hat on the beats with your foot, so it is not necessary to also strike the hi-hat cymbals with your stick (but you can if you want to). Pattern 5 is a "reverse disco" beat; you will close the hi-hat on the upbeats with your foot.

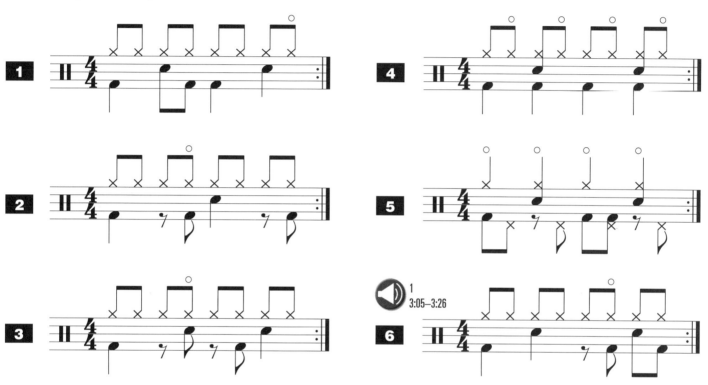

**Cross-stick:** Using a cross-stick technique on the snare drum, as illustrated in the photo, produces a fat "click" sound. Experiment to find the place on your drumstick that produces the best sound. When you find that "sweet spot" on the shoulder of the stick, draw a line around it with a felt marker so you have a visual reference point when trying to nail the cross-stick. This technique is especially effective on slow songs (ballads).

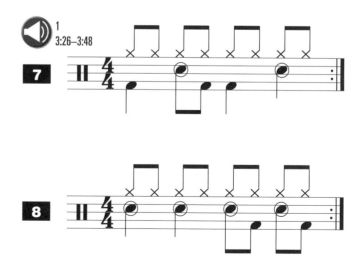

**Snare Ride:** Instead of riding on the hi-hat or cymbal, you can play straight 8th notes all on the snare drum, accenting the backbeats on 2 and 4. Pattern 9, in which you alternate the sticking, is especially good for fast tempos. On pattern 10, ride on the snare drum with the right hand, just as you would on the ride cymbal, and continue to play backbeats on the snare drum with the left hand.

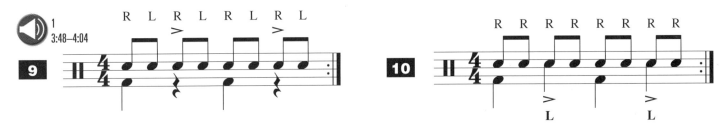

## Tom-tom Beats

Substituting tom-toms for snare drum notes can add color to a pattern, as in the examples below.

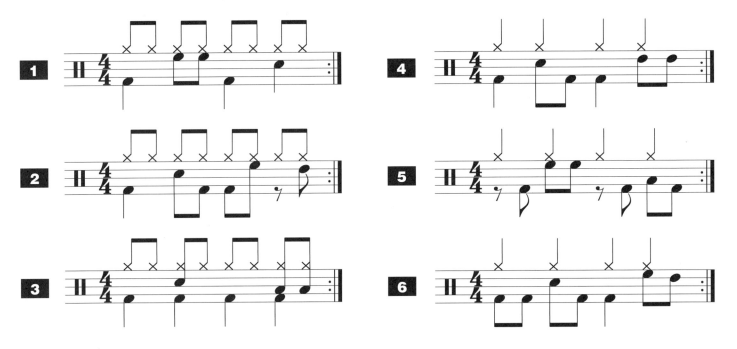

Riding on the floor tom produces a very powerful sound. For clarity in the examples below, the floor tom notes are written on a separate staff.

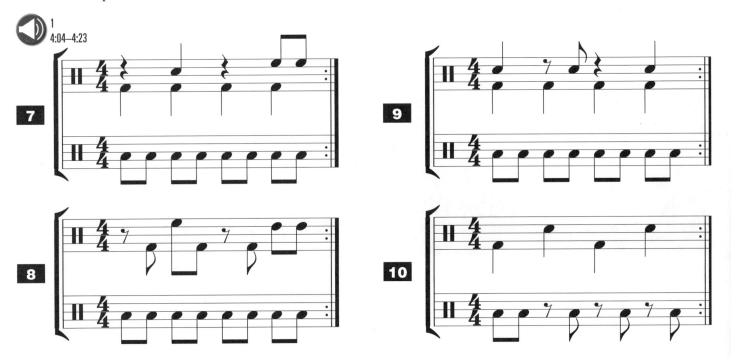

# Odd-time Beats

The following patterns are basic examples of "odd-time" beats, which have been used in the music of such 1960s and '70s prog bands as Yes, ELP, Jethro Tull, and Genesis, and more recently by Rush, Dream Theater, Porcupine Tree, and Opeth, among others. Rockers Led Zeppelin have a fair amount of interesting odd-time songs, as do jam bands the Allman Brothers and the Grateful Dead. More recent artists who occasionally dabble in odd-times are Sting, Soundgarden, the Toadies, Radiohead, and Alice in Chains. Following are just a few sample odd-time beats to get you started.

## Two-bar Patterns

Playing a two-bar pattern can add interest to a song. In pattern 8, you can hold the open hi-hat note for its full value, not closing it until beat 1 of the following bar, or you can close it on the & of 4.

# 8th-note Fills

The examples below consist of basic 8th-note fills around the snare drum and tom-toms. First, practice each one individually so that you can play it smoothly. Then, using the chart at the top of the page as a guide, play a beat for three bars, then play one of the fills, then go back into the beat for three more bars, play a fill, and so on. Make sure you do not speed up or slow down the 8th notes when you play the fill.

Follow the same procedure on the next page with 3-beat and 2-beat fills. Feel free to substitute other beats for the beats provided in the charts at the top of each section.

## 4-beat Fills

Begin all fills with the right hand and alternate, unless otherwise indicated.

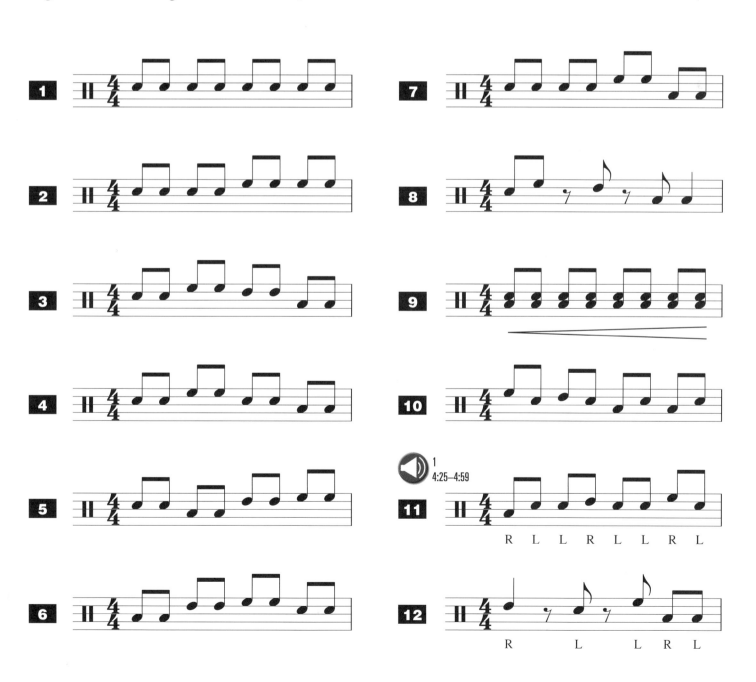

## 3-beat Fills

## 2-beat Fills

## 8th-note Fills with Bass Drum

The following fills incorporate bass drum along with the snare and tom-toms. The fills on this page should be practiced the same way as the fills on page 27; play a beat for three bars, then play a fill on the fourth bar.

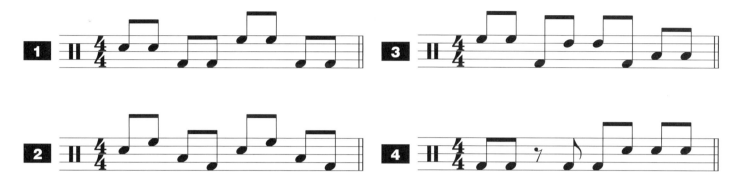

## 8th-note Fills with Flams and Bass Drum

A flam is played on a single drum with the two sticks hitting almost at the same time, but just far enough apart to make the note sound "fatter." It should not sound like two separate notes.

## 8th-note Fills with Flat Flams and Bass Drum

Flat flams are played by hitting two different drums at exactly the same time.

Here are some additional fill patterns using bass drum, flams, and flat flams.

# Musical Form

Songs are broken up into sections with names such as Introduction (or Intro), Verse, Chorus, and Bridge. Each section is usually made up of phrases. You could think of phrases as sentences and sections as paragraphs, which often conforms to the way the lyrics are arranged in songs.

You can usually follow the form of the song by listening to what the other instruments are playing. A different section will sound different in some way—usually because the melody and/or chords (harmony) will be different. Good drummers are aware of the form of each tune they play and will mark the form of the tune with fills, cymbal crashes, different beats, and different sounds.

## Four-bar Phrases

A common phrase length in rock and blues is four measures, so we will begin by developing a feel for playing four-bar phrases. The first step is to be able to hit a cymbal crash on the first beat of every four-bar phrase, as illustrated below.

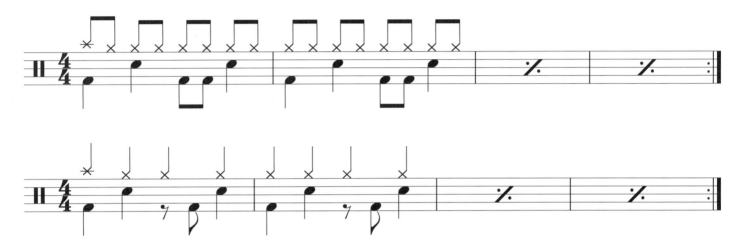

When playing with an 8th-note feel, especially at fast tempos, you can wait until the second beat to resume the hi-hat or ride cymbal after playing a cymbal crash on the first beat, as the sound of the crash will drown out anything you played on the "&" of the first beat anyway.

Using the above examples as guides, play along with audio tracks 3, 5, 7, and 9, striking the crash cymbal on the first beat of each four-bar phrase. Once you are comfortable with the examples above, try playing with the same tracks using a variety of beats from the previous pages of the book until you can "feel" a four-bar phrase without having to concentrate too hard on counting measures. Each audio track begins with four cowbell notes that give you the quarter-note tempo for that track.

# Blues Form

Audio tracks 2 through 7 each feature a basic 12-bar blues—a structure that many blues, rock, pop, and jazz songs are built on. The 12 bars are made up of three, four-bar phrases.

Typical blues lyrics are similar on the first two phrases and different on the third, such as:

| | |
|---|---|
| **phrase 1:** | Well I woke up this mornin', and I felt so bad |
| **phrase 2:** | I said I woke up this mornin', and you know I felt so bad |
| **phrase 3:** | My baby went and left me, and now I'm burnin' mad |

## Slow Blues

On audio track 2 the following drum pattern is played all the way through. Notice the cymbal crash at the beginning of each four-bar phrase.

Using the chart below as a guide, play along to audio track 3, which is the same as track 2 except that there is no drum part. As a guide, you will hear a cowbell playing quarter notes, a shaker playing 8th notes, and a tambourine playing backbeats. At first, try using the beat that was used on track 2, but then try a variety of different beats from Chapter One. Remember to play a cymbal crash at the beginning of each four-bar phrase. On the track, the 12-bar phrase is played twice.

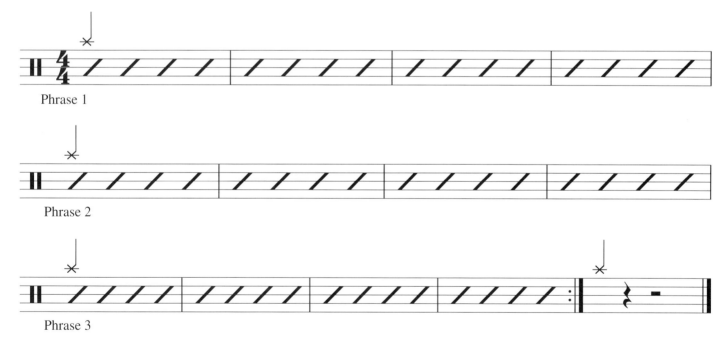

Phrase 1

Phrase 2

Phrase 3

## Medium Blues

When playing blues songs, drummers will often change the "color" by switching from hi-hat to ride cymbal. But this should only be done at logical times. For example, you might use the hi-hat when the singer is singing, switch to ride cymbal during the guitar solo, and switch back to hi-hat when the singer starts up again. You will usually make the switch at the beginning of a 12-bar section.

Audio track 4 is another blues, performed at a slightly faster tempo. The following beat is played throughout the track, with the ride pattern played on hi-hat the first time through and on ride cymbal the second time.

Audio track 5 is the same as track 4, except with no drums. You can play along to it using the same chart as a guide that you used with audio track 3. Again, you will hear a cowbell playing quarter notes, a shaker playing 8th notes, and a tambourine playing backbeats as a guide. After you are comfortable playing the beat that is used on track 4, try other beats of your own choice. Remember to switch from hi-hat to ride cymbal when the song repeats.

##  Riff Blues

A good way to emphasize the return to the beginning of each 12-bar phrase (the "top") is to lead into the cymbal crash at the beginning of measure 1 by playing a fill in measure 12, as you will hear on audio track 6. You'll hear the following drum pattern throughout the track, with cymbal crashes at the beginning of each four-bar phrase.

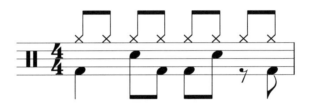

In measure 12, fill 1 (below left) is played the first time through, and fill 2 (below right) is played the second time.

Audio track 7 is the same as track 6, but without drums. Try playing along with it using the beat and fill that were used on track 6, and then try other beats and fills of your choice, using the chart below as a guide.

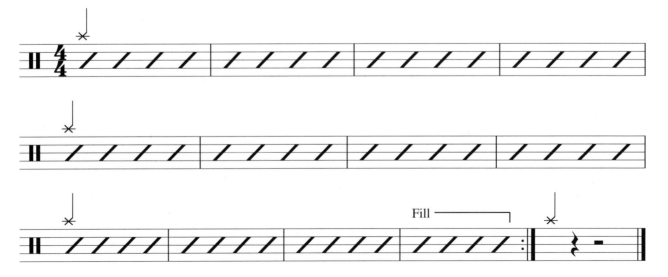

# Verse/Chorus Structure

Many songs alternate between verses and choruses. Generally, the lyrics for each verse will be different, but the lyrics for all of the choruses will be the same.

The music for the verses will usually be different than the chorus music. Therefore, the drummer will often play something different during the verses than what is played during the choruses. You still want it to sound like the same song, though, so you don't want to change the beat too much. In fact, sometimes you don't change the beat at all; you just change the way it sounds. A common way to do this is to play the same bass drum and snare drum part on both, but ride on the hi-hat during the verses and switch to ride cymbal during the choruses.

## Verse/Chorus Form

Audio track 8 features a short song written in a verse/chorus framework. Each section is eight measures long. The following two-bar pattern is played throughout. During the verses, the quarter-note ride is played on hi-hat; on the choruses, it switches to the bell of the ride cymbal.

Track 9 is the same as track 8, except without drums. Play along with the track, using the following chart as a guide. First, try using the same beat that was played on track 8. Then, try one- or two-measure beats of your choice, riding on the hi-hat during the verses and riding on the ride cymbal during the choruses.

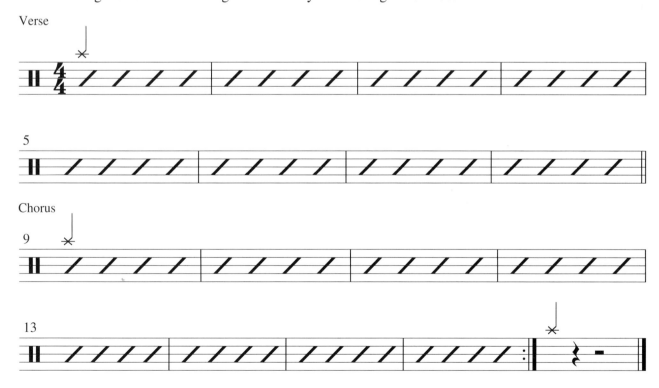

An effective way to make a change between the verses and choruses is to play the same thing on the bass and snare drums for both but change the feel on the hi-hat or ride cymbal, as in the following examples.

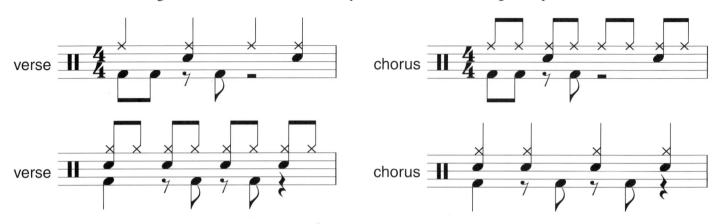

You can also combine changing the feel with changing the sound. In the following example, the quarter-note feel in the verse is played on hi-hat, while the 8th-note feel in the chorus is played on ride cymbal.

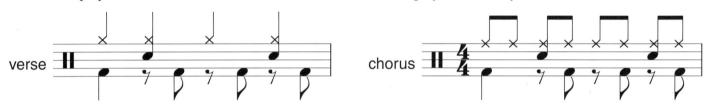

Another approach is to change the beat slightly. The following beats are related, so that it sounds like you are still playing the same song, but different enough to provide variety between the verse and chorus sections.

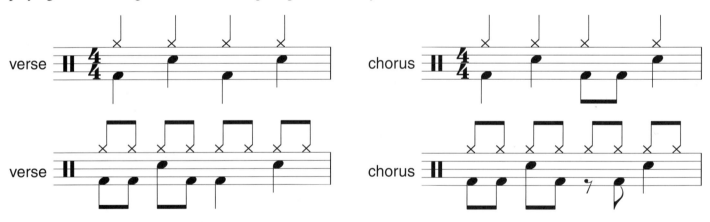

Switching from a half-time feel (created by playing the snare drum on beat 3) in the verse to a standard backbeat feel in the chorus can also be effective, as shown in the following examples.

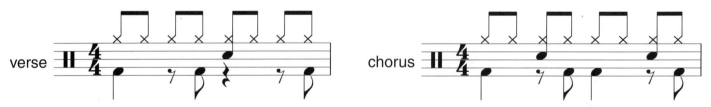

Play along with audio track 9 using all of the above suggestions. Then use other beats of your choice from the preceding pages, applying the same ideas.

# "Dusk"

The drum part on track 10 reflects the structure of the tune by changing the beat and the sound between the verse and chorus sections. The verses feature a hi-hat ride with a single snare drum cross-stick on beat 4. During the choruses, backbeats are played between the snare on beat 2 and alternating toms on beat 4, creating a two-bar pattern, and the ride pattern moves to cymbal. The bass drum remains consistent. The following chart is the exact drum part from track 10.

Track 11 features the same song as track 10, but without drums. Play along with it following the drum part from track 10. Then feel free to come up with your own drum part using different patterns and ideas from Chapter One.

## "Purple Rainbow"

Verses and choruses can be arranged in different ways. The structure of the tune on track 12 is chorus/verse/chorus/verse/chorus. Again, the drum part is slightly different between the two sections. The choruses feature a two-bar pattern with ride cymbal. The verses use a one-bar pattern, which is the first bar of the two-bar pattern used in the chorus sections. The ride switches to hi-hat for a "color" change. The following chart is the exact drum part from track 12.

Track 13 features the same song as track 12, but without drums. Play along with it following the drum part notated above. Then create your own drum part using different patterns and ideas from Chapter One.

# "Up from the Depths"

14

This song is in a verse/chorus format. The first verse takes a "slow build" approach, beginning with just the bass drum playing four-on-the-floor, and the snare backbeat entering midway through the verse. A syncopated floor-tom ride pattern is played in the second and third verses. The chorus consists of a straight-four snare groove, with flammed snare and kick reinforcing some of the guitar licks.

15

Track 15 is the same as track 14 except without drums. Play along with it following the drum part from track 14. Then feel free to come up with your own drum part using different patterns and ideas from Chapter One.

## "High Five"

**16**

Because this song is in 5/4, you will hear a five-note count-off at the beginning, which sets the pace. This song follows a verse/chorus format in which the verse groove consists of a one-measure kick/snare pattern, with an 8th-note ride pattern played on closed hi-hat. The chorus groove consists of a two-measure kick/snare pattern, with a quarter-note ride pattern played on the bell of the ride cymbal.

**17**

Track 17 is the same as track 16 except without drums. Play along with it following the drum part from track 16. Then feel free to come up with your own drum part using different 5/4 grooves from page 23.

# CHAPTER TWO
## 16th-note Beats

In this chapter, we will look at beats and fills that use 16th notes. Just as 8th notes divide each quarter-note beat in half, 16th notes divide each quarter-note beat into fourths. They are counted as in the example below.

Many rhythmic figures combine 8th and 16th notes (or rests). The following examples show how these rhythms relate to straight 16ths.

When a dot is placed after a note, the note's value increases by one-half. For example, a quarter note is worth two 8th notes; a dotted-quarter is worth three 8th notes. An 8th note is worth two 16th notes; a dotted-8th is worth three 16ths. The example below illustrates several common patterns that combine a dotted-8th note (or rest) with a 16th note (or rest).

The patterns on the following pages combine quarter notes, 8th notes, and 16th notes. When first learning beats that have 8th-note or quarter-note ride patterns, it is important to count straight 16ths (1 e & a 2 e & a etc.) throughout the pattern so that any notes that fall between the 8ths or quarters are placed accurately.

Sometimes the same snare drum rhythms can look very different even though they sound the same, depending on whether the snare drum part is notated with the bass drum part or with the hi-hat/cymbal part. The following two examples are played exactly the same way.

When riding on the ride cymbal, or on any other element of the drumset besides the hi-hat, you can use the left foot on the hi-hat pedal to keep a quarter-note pulse, as in the example at lower left, or to reinforce the backbeat, as in the example at lower right. Adding a fourth element of coordination can take time, so be patient.

Listen to audio track 18 to hear how selected patterns from this chapter should sound. Once you are comfortable with the patterns on a page, try playing them along with tracks 20 and 22.

## Chapter Two Recorded Examples

18

Audio track 18 features several examples from Chapter Two to give you an overview of the types of patterns you will be learning. For convenience, each of the patterns played on track 18 is notated below.

16th-note Ride Pattern 4b (page 41)

a 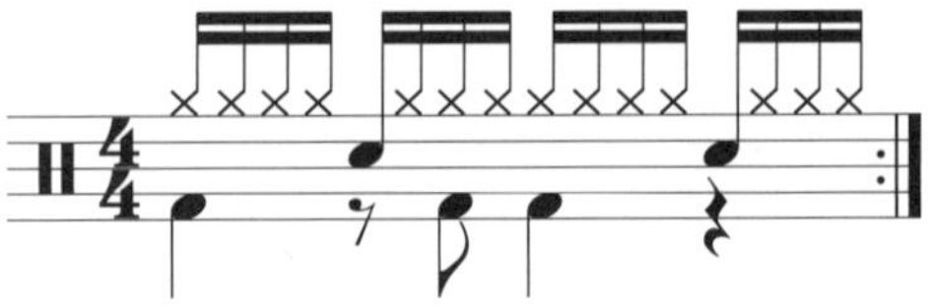

Bass and Snare Variation 9b (page 45)

b 

Bass and Snare Variation 21a (page 46)

c 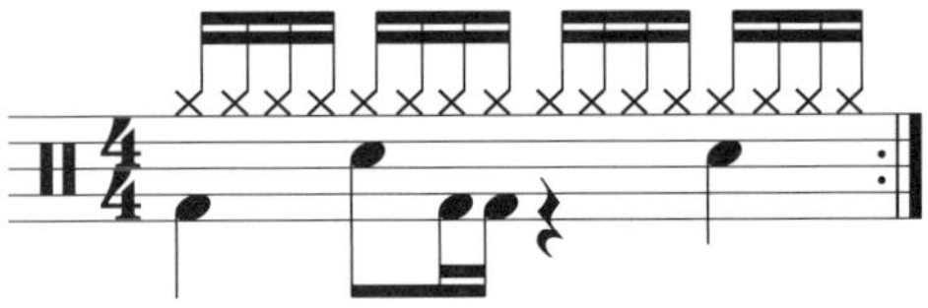

Bass and Snare Variation 60b (page 51)

d 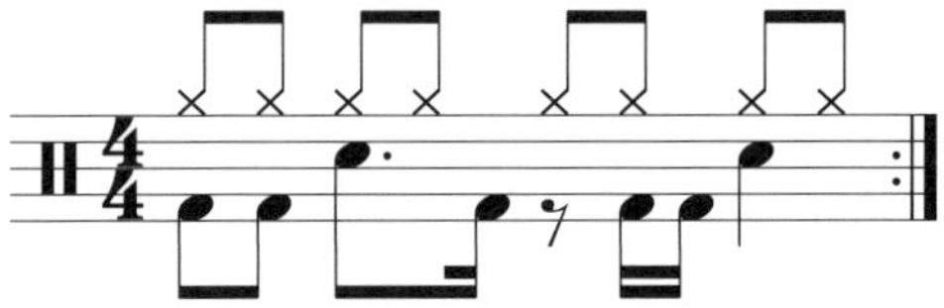

Alternating Ride with Variations 11 (page 53)

e 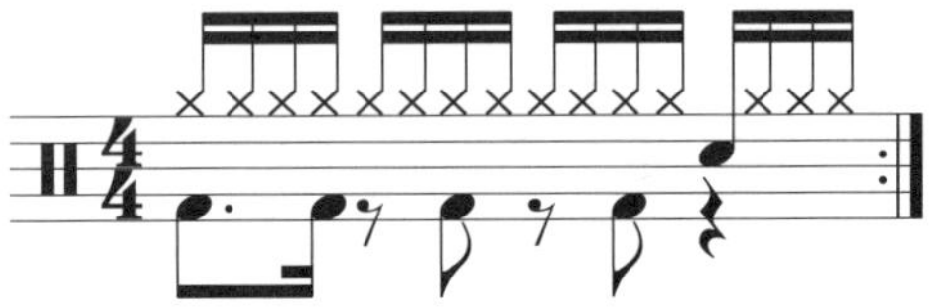

Straight-four Snare Drum 6a (page 55)

f 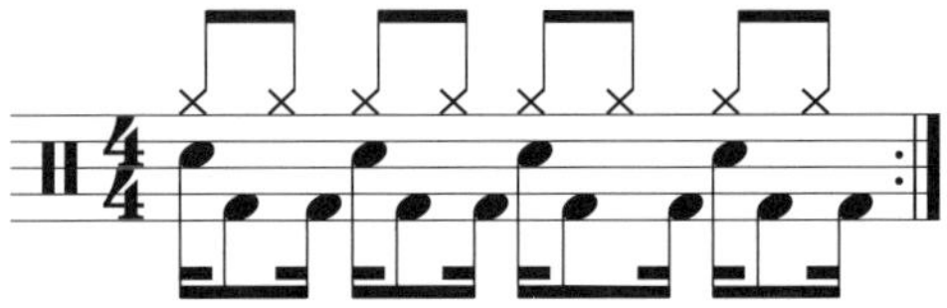

Two-bar Pattern 3 (page 57)

g 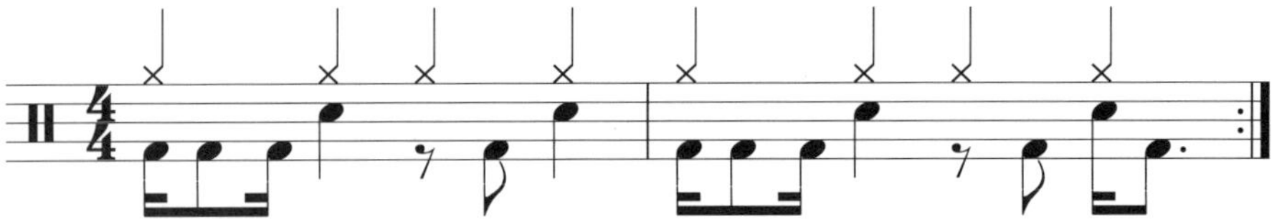

Two-bar Pattern 5 (page 57)

h 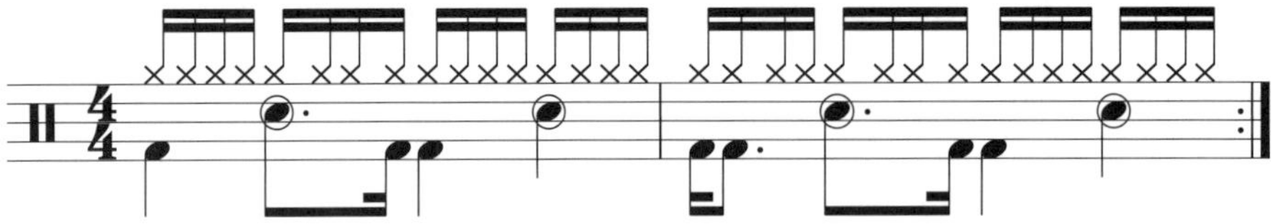

Two-bar Pattern 16 (page 59)

i 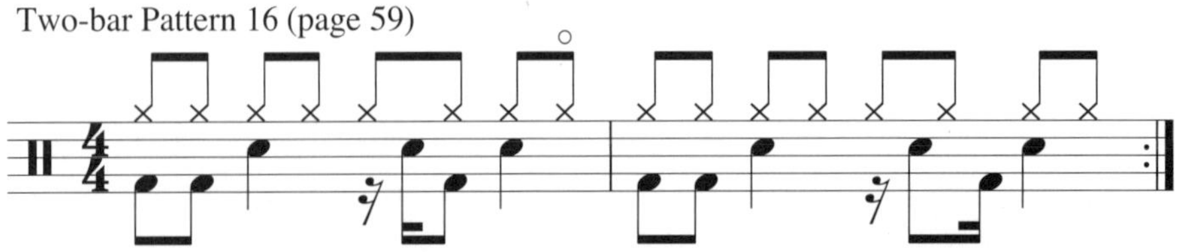

Two-bar Pattern 21 (page 59)

j 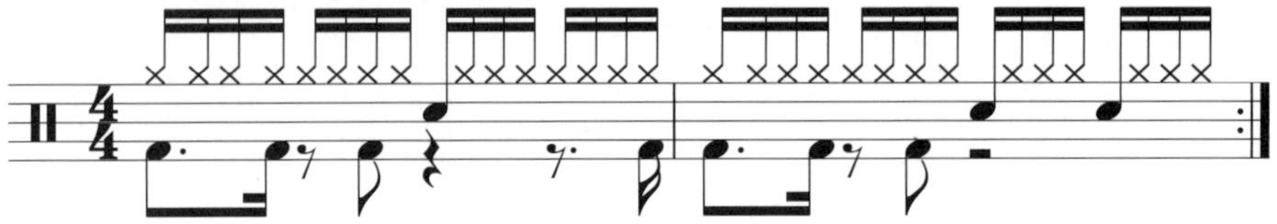

## 16th-note Ride Patterns

The examples on the next three pages feature 16th-note ride patterns with quarter-note and 8th-note patterns in the snare drum and bass drum. The ride patterns on the left side of the page are meant to be played with one hand on either ride cymbal or hi-hat, while the other hand plays snare drum. The patterns on the right side of the page are to be played on hi-hat, using alternating hands as shown in example 1b. Whether playing the 16th-note ride with one hand or with alternating hands, you can play all the notes at the same volume, you can accent 1 & 2 & 3 & 4 &, playing the e's and a's softer, or you can accent the quarter-note pulse (1, 2, 3, 4).

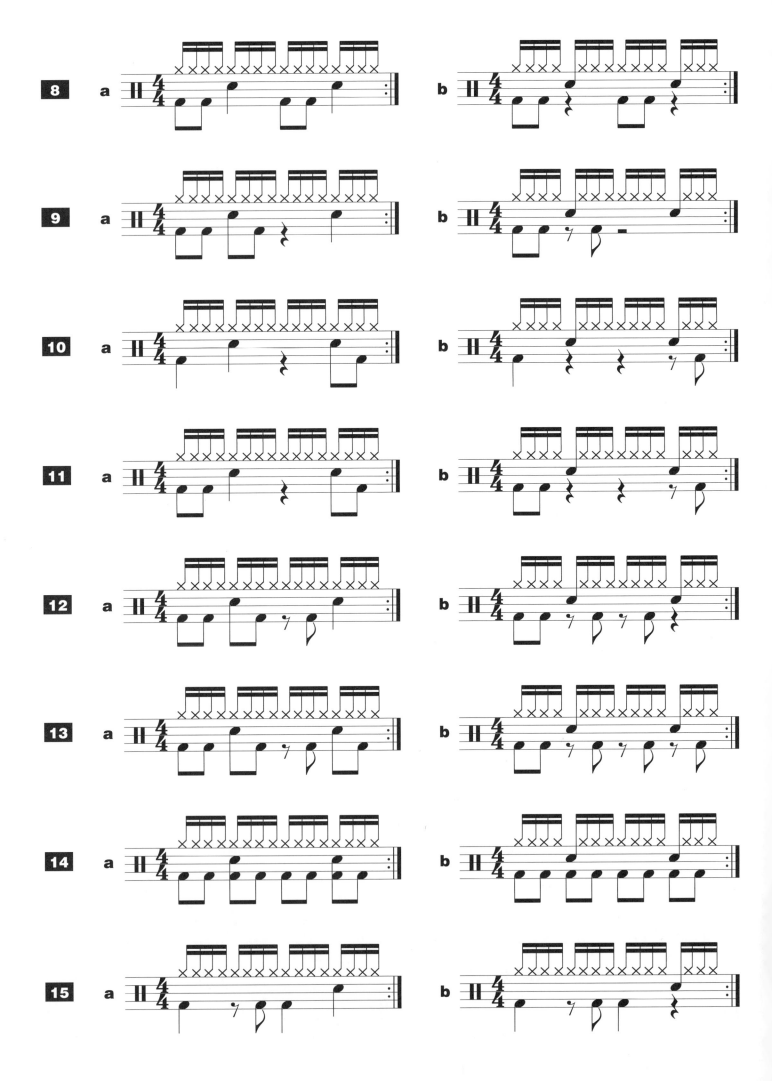

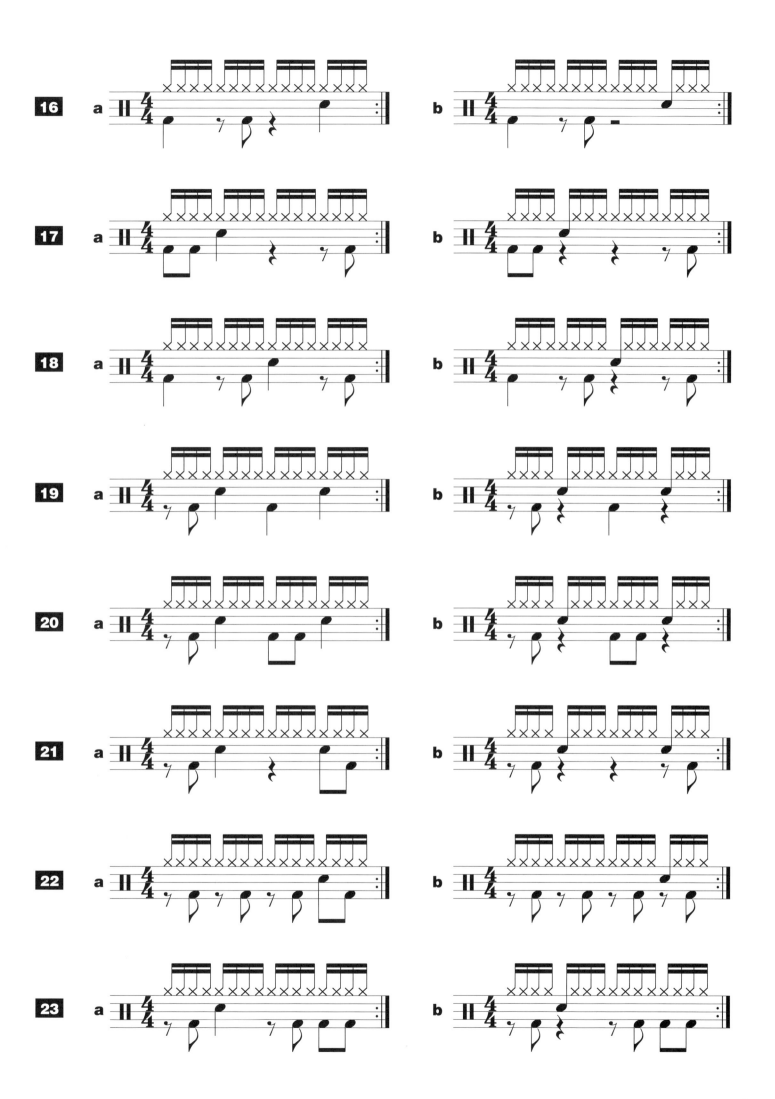

# Bass and Snare Variations

The following pages contain a variety of beats using 16th notes. The left-hand columns feature 16th-note ride patterns, while the right-hand columns feature 8th-note ride patterns. Each pattern can be played while riding on either the hi-hat or the ride cymbal. As you go across the page, the snare and bass parts stay the same while the ride pattern changes from 16ths to 8ths.

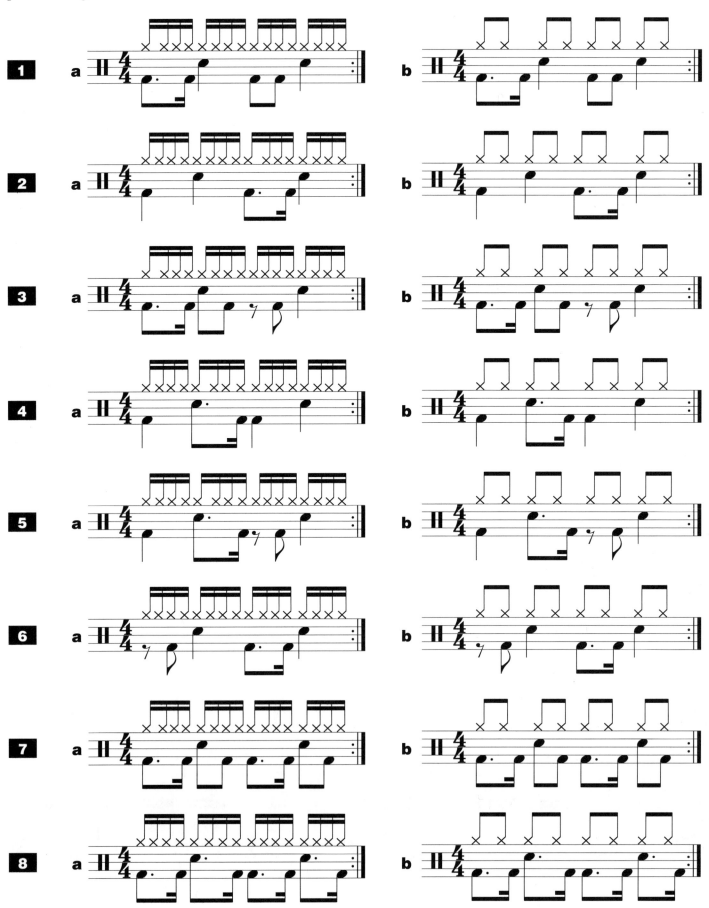

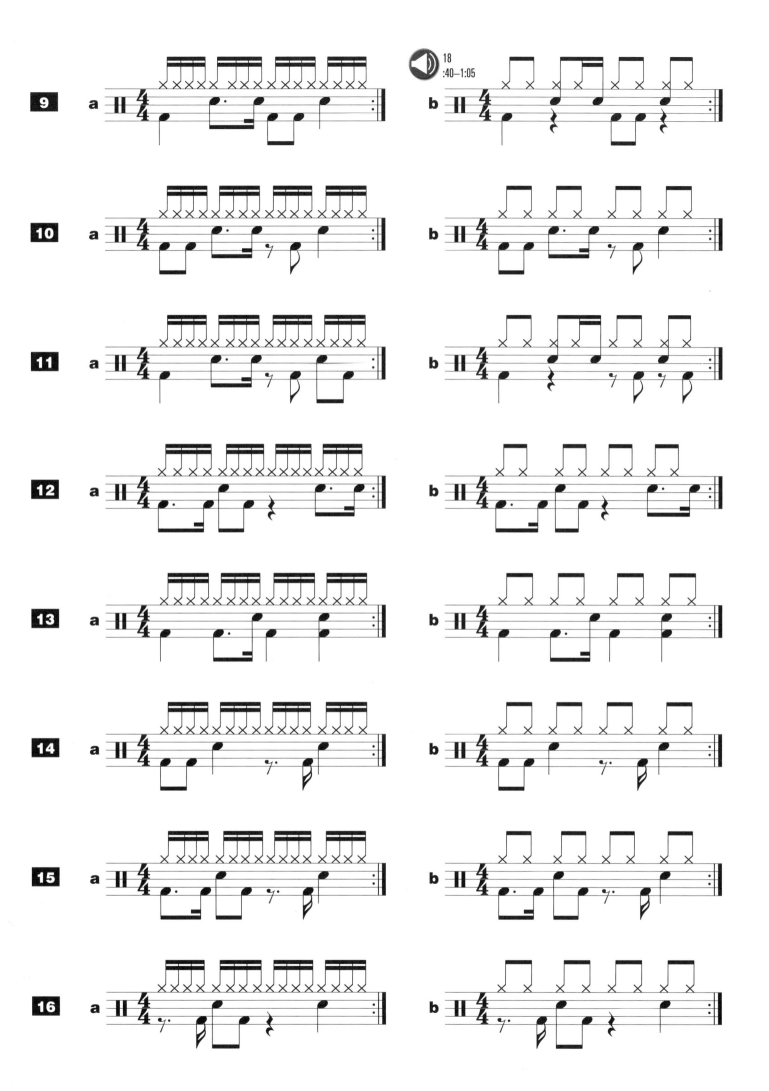

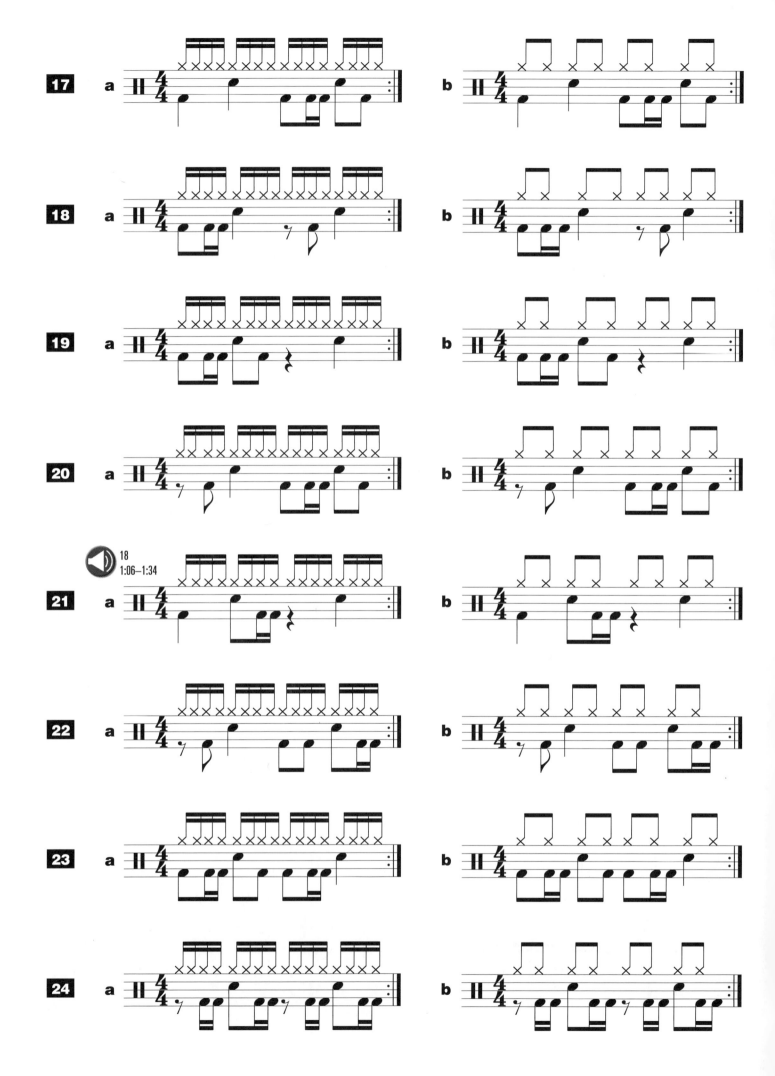

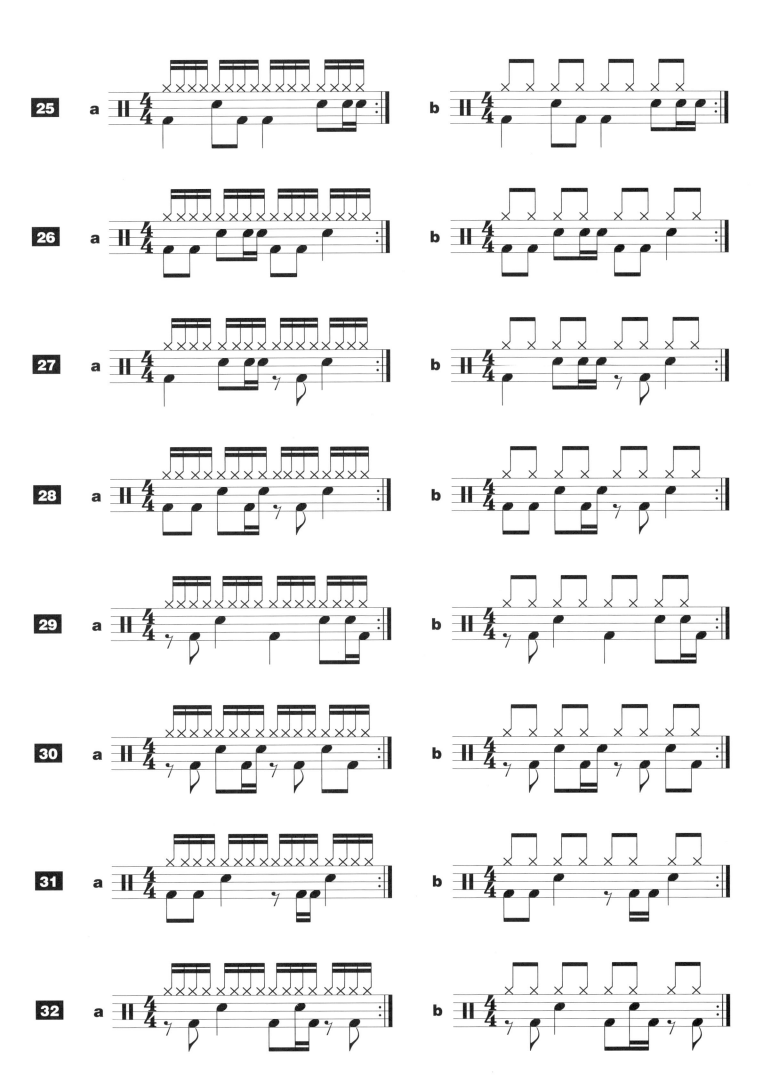

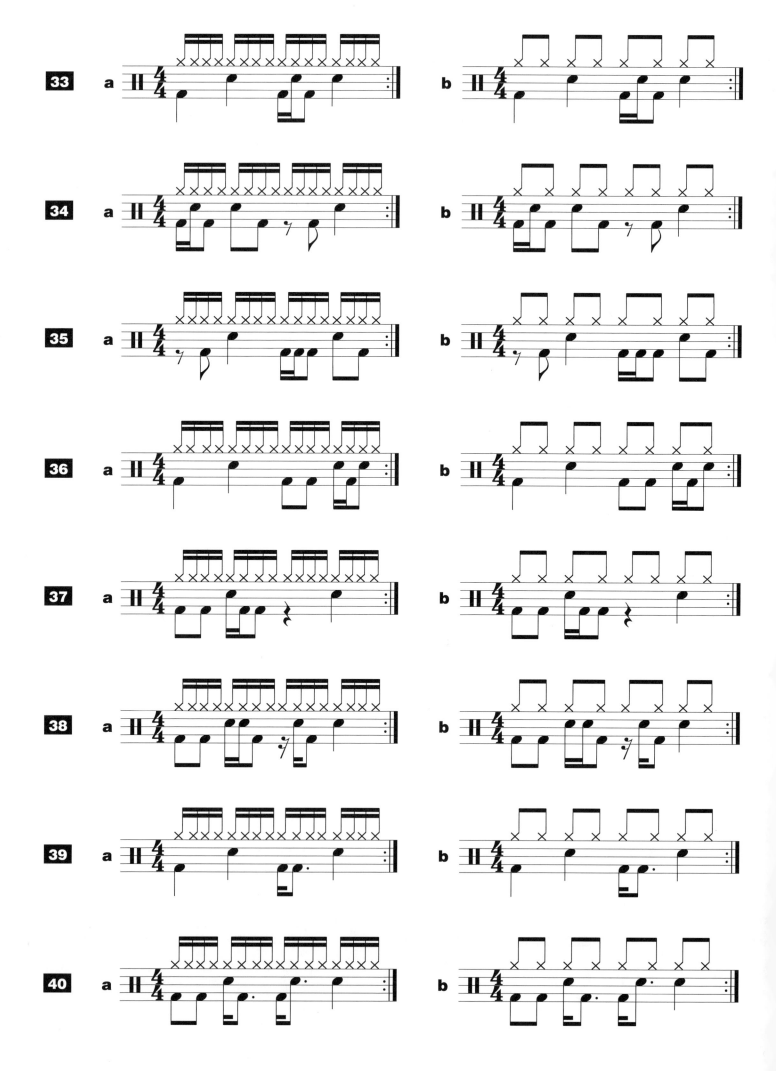

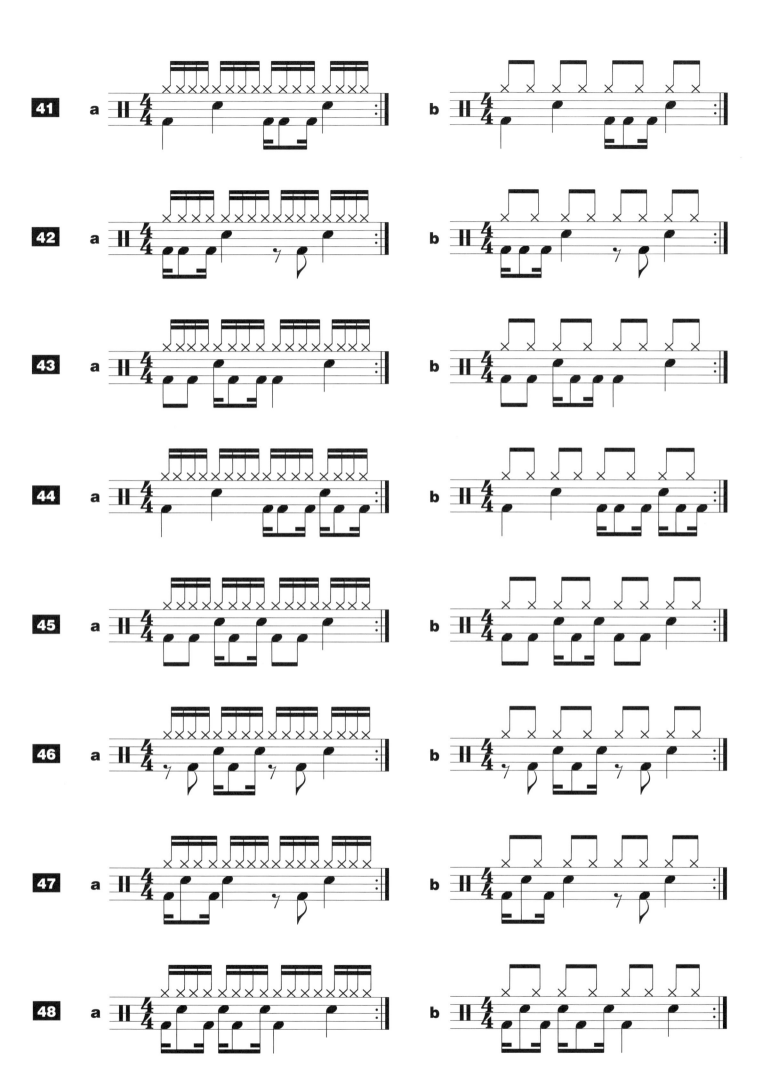

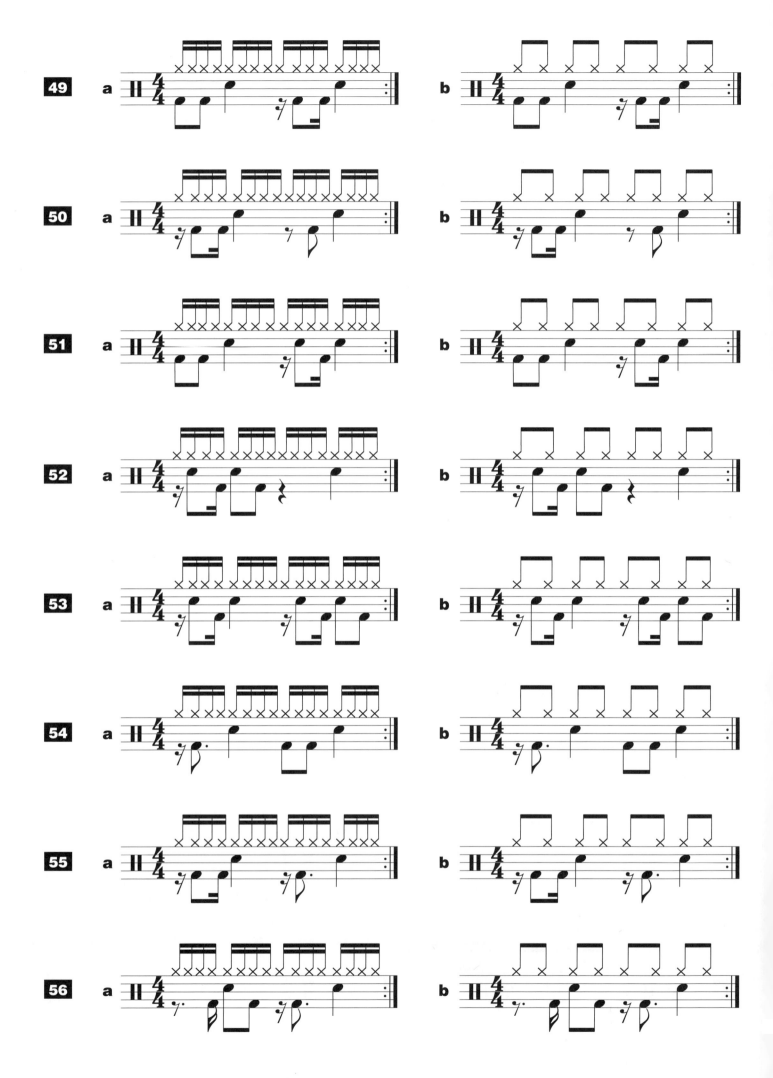

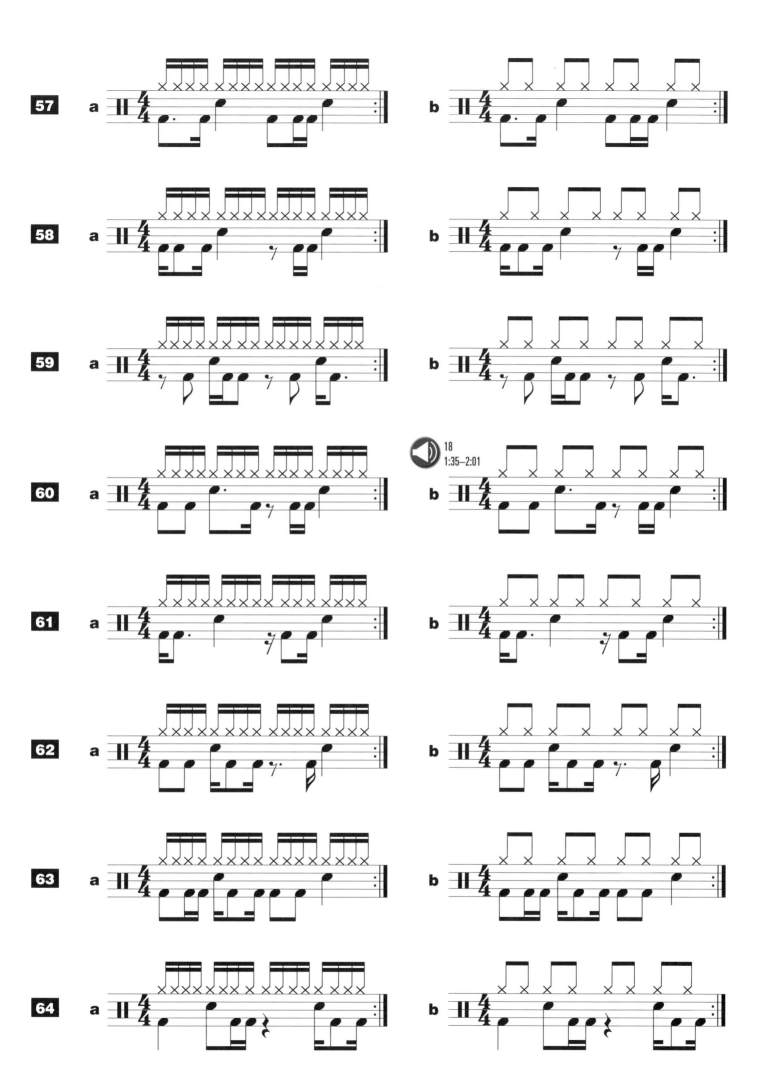

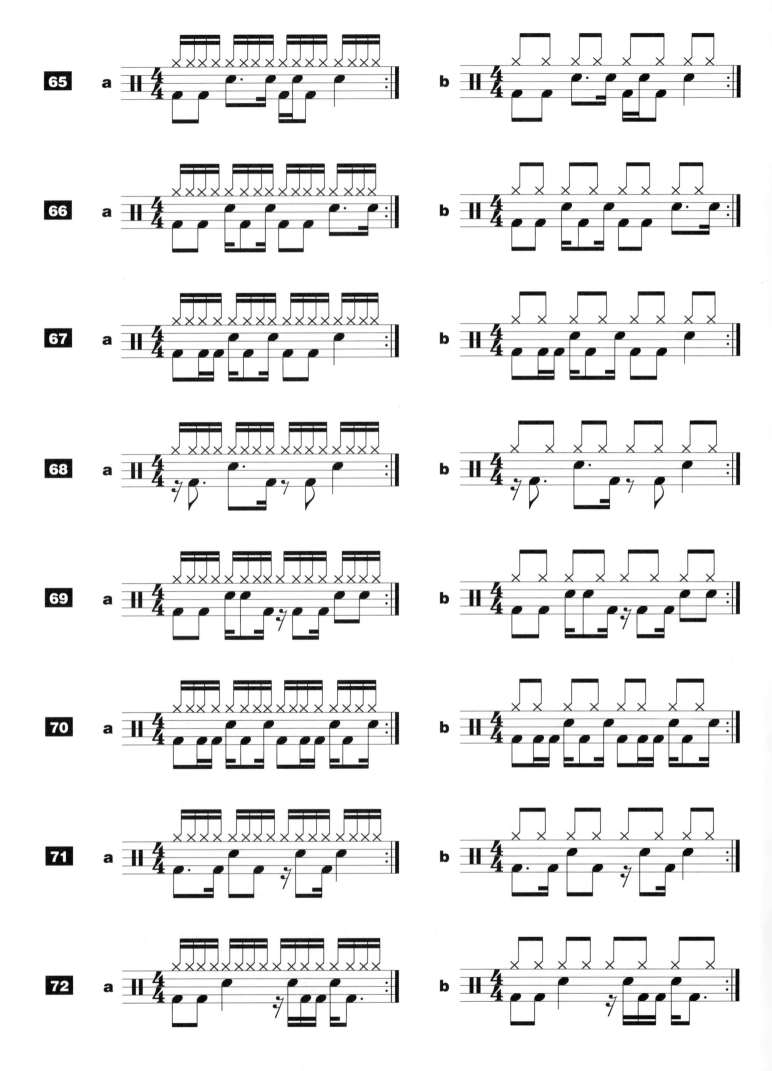

# Alternating Ride with Variations

On the following patterns, be especially careful when coordinating bass drum notes with left-hand hi-hat notes. Develop precision before trying for speed.

## 16ths with Quarter-note Ride

When first learning these patterns, it is a good idea to count straight 16ths (1e&a 2e&a 3e&a 4e&a) throughout so that you place all notes accurately. Examples 15 and 16 displace the quarter-note ride by an 8th note so the ride is played on the offbeats. Playing just the "&"s is sometimes called an upbeat or offbeat ride pattern.

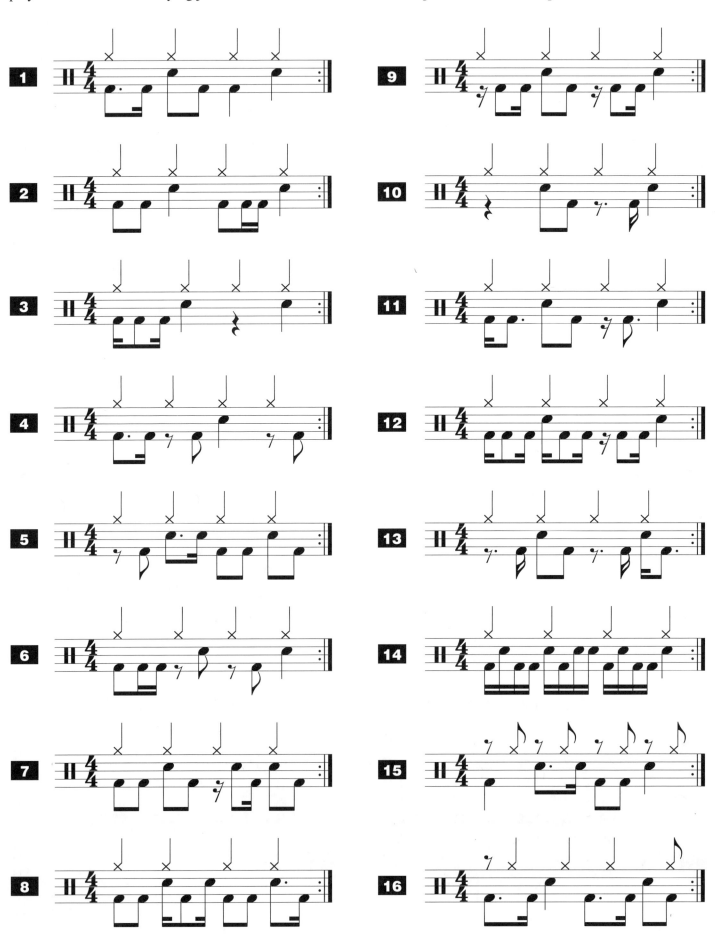

## Straight-four Snare Drum

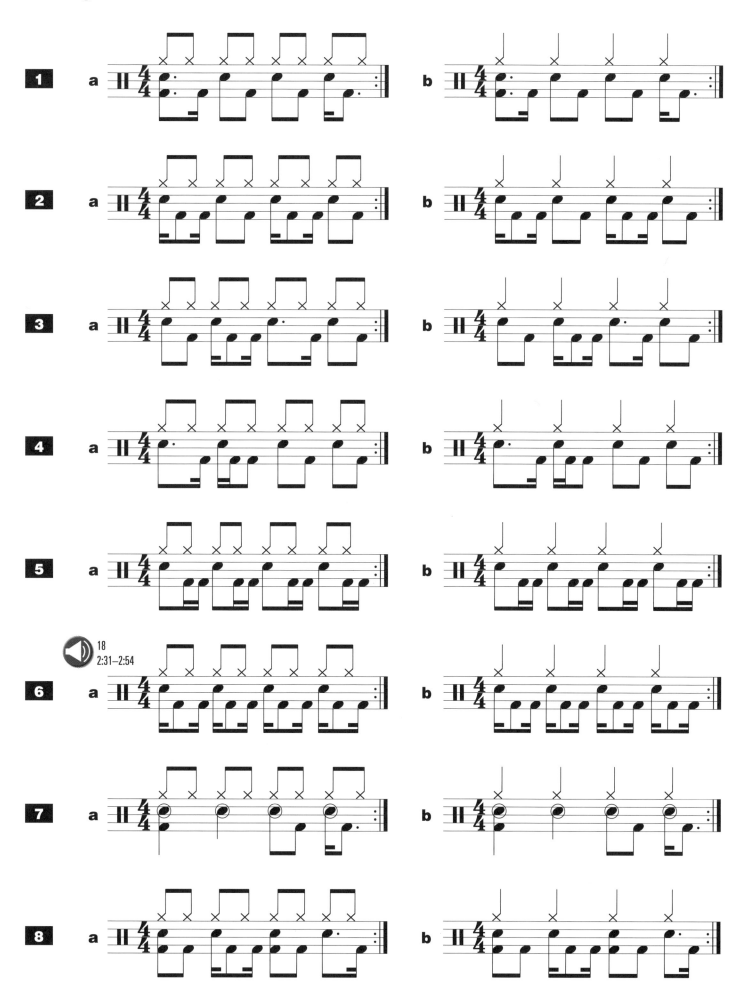

## Tom-tom Beats

On patterns 1 and 2, play the accented notes a lot louder than the unaccented ones for the best effect. Pattern 4 shows how to use the floor tom and bass drum to simulate a double-bass effect.

## Open Hi-hat Beats

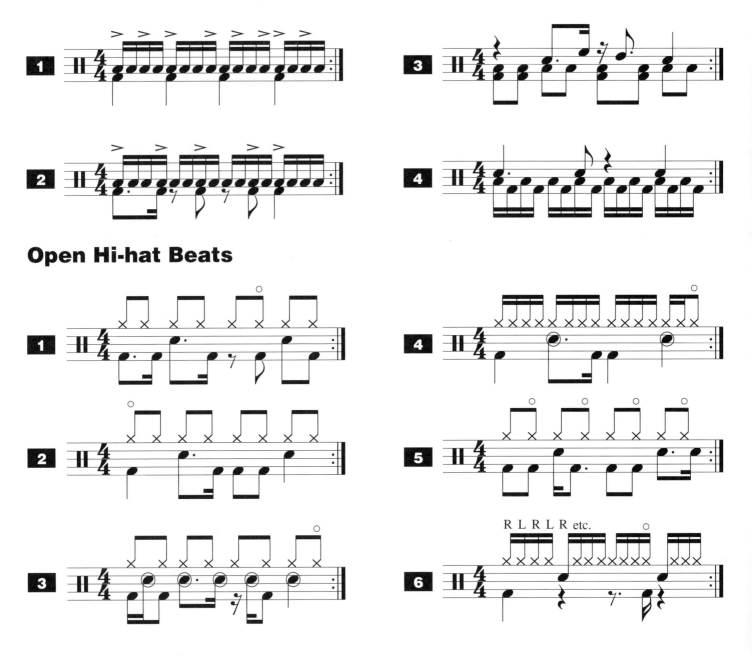

## Double-bass Beats

A lot of the patterns in this chapter can be applied to double-bass drums or a double-bass pedal. Often, double-bass players keep up a steady flow of 16ths, as in the patterns below. The second bass drum (or left pedal) is written on the bottom line of the staff.

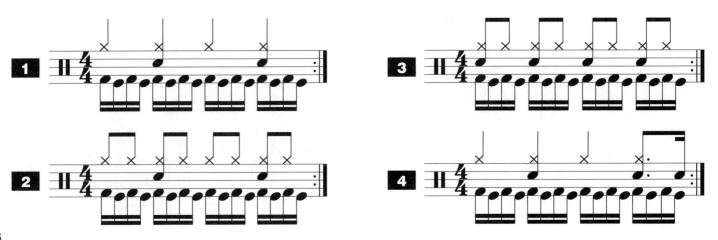

## Two-bar Patterns

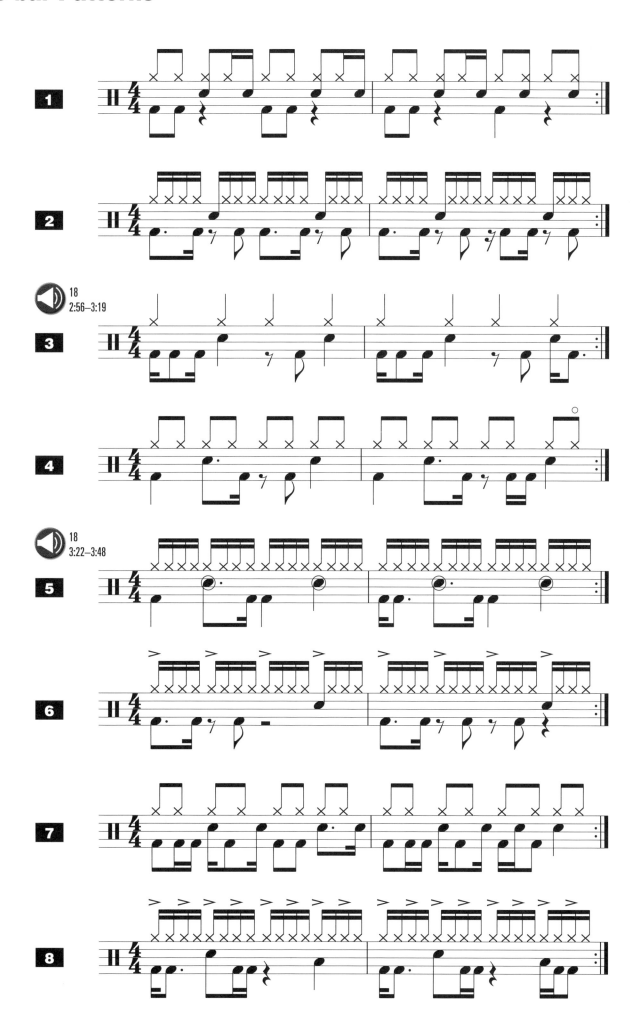

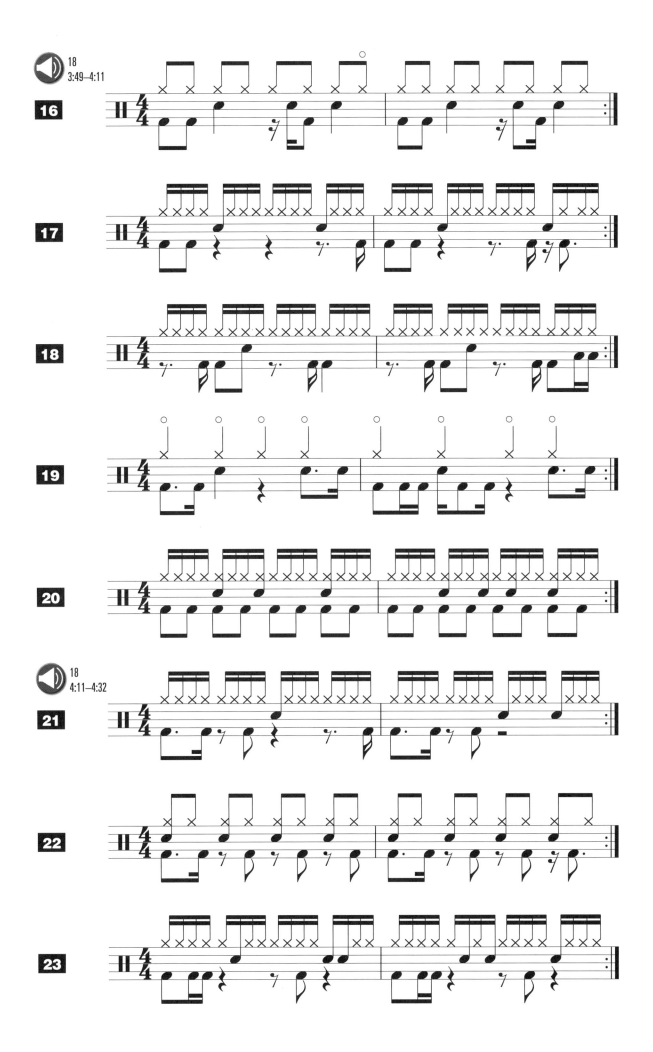

# 16th-note Fills

The patterns on this page and the next consist of basic 16th-note fills starting on beats 1, 2, 3, and 4. First, practice each fill individually so that you can play it smoothly. Then, practice each fill in context using the 16th-feel and 8th-feel charts at the top of this page as guides. Feel free to substitute different beats for the ones notated in the charts.

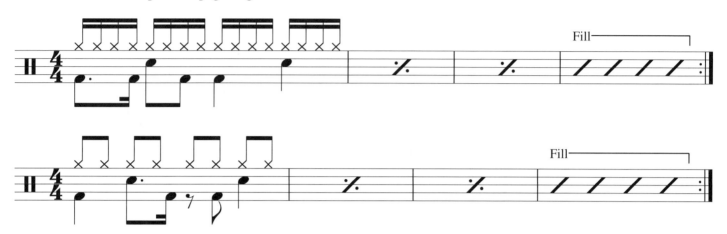

## 4-beat Fills

## 3-beat Fills

## 2-beat Fills

## 1-beat Fills

The following fills incorporate the bass drum, flams, and flat flams. Practice them with the four-bar charts at the top of page 60 (three bars of a beat followed by the fill bar).

## 4-beat Fills

**25**

**29**

Paradiddle

**26**

R L R R L R L L R L R R L R L L

**30**

**27**

R L L R L L R L L R L L R L

**31**

**28**

**32**

## 3-beat Fills

**33**

**34**

## 2-beat Fills

**35**

**36**

## 1-beat Fills

**37**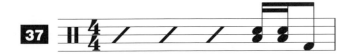

**38**

## Slow Verse/Chorus Form

**19** Audio track 19 features a slow 16th-note groove. The song is in a verse/chorus structure, with each section consisting of four measures. The piece is played twice through. The chart below shows the drum part that was played on track 19. Notice that the verse features a cross-stick sound on the snare drum. The playing is more aggressive on the chorus, and the bass drum part is slightly different. The beginning of each section is marked with a cymbal crash.

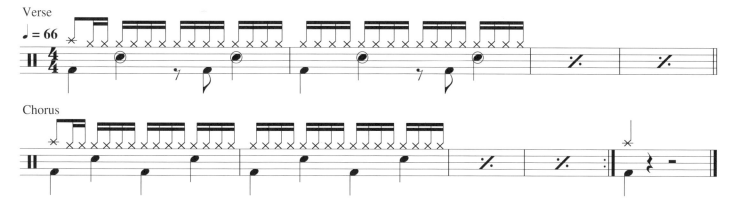

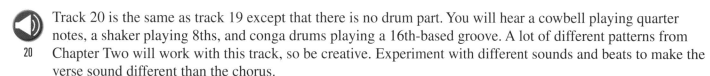

**20** Track 20 is the same as track 19 except that there is no drum part. You will hear a cowbell playing quarter notes, a shaker playing 8ths, and conga drums playing a 16th-based groove. A lot of different patterns from Chapter Two will work with this track, so be creative. Experiment with different sounds and beats to make the verse sound different than the chorus.

## Funk Blues

**21** Audio track 21 features a 16th-based funk blues. The same pattern is played throughout, with a cymbal crash marking the beginning of each 4-bar phrase. The following chart shows the exact drum part that was played on track 21.

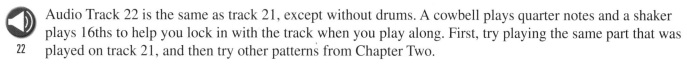

**22** Audio Track 22 is the same as track 21, except without drums. A cowbell plays quarter notes and a shaker plays 16ths to help you lock in with the track when you play along. First, try playing the same part that was played on track 21, and then try other patterns from Chapter Two.

# Musical Form, Part Two

## Intros

Many songs begin with an introduction or "intro." Usually the music in the intro will be similar to, or even the same as, the music in the verses or choruses, but it can also be different. In a song that has vocals, the intro is often played instrumentally and serves to establish the overall feel of the song.

Sometimes you will play the same beat for the intro that you are going to use for the verses and/or choruses of the song. Other times you will only play part of the complete pattern. For example, you might leave out the ride pattern during the intro and play only the bass drum and snare drum beat. Then again, you might leave out the drums and just establish the ride pattern on hi-hat or cymbal. You can play any single element of the kit (snare drum only, bass drum only, etc.) or any combination of elements. Another option is to play the same beat that you are going to use in the song, but change the "color" by playing it on different parts of the kit (for example, riding on the floor tom during the intro and then switching to cymbal or hi-hat when the first verse begins).

In some cases, you might play something completely different during the intro than you are going to play in the rest of the song. But keep in mind that the intro is supposed to "introduce" the song, so the part you play during the intro should, in some way, prepare listeners for what is to come, even if you are simply going to establish the basic pulse by playing quarter notes on the hi-hat, which brings us to the next song.

### "Big Foot"

**23** Audio track 23 contains a song written in the verse/chorus form, which has a four-bar intro. On the recording, the drum part for the intro consists only of quarter notes on the hi-hat. A short fill at the end of the fourth measure leads into the first verse. The verses feature a 16th-note ride pattern that is played on the hi-hat with alternating hands, with a single snare drum hit on beat four of each measure. During the choruses the ride pattern switches to 8th notes on the ride cymbal. The bass drum moves to a 2-bar pattern while the snare drum goes to straight backbeats. The chart on the next page illustrates the exact drum part that is played on track 23.

## Pickups and Lead-ins

Sometimes a tune will start a beat or two before the first beat of the first complete measure. Such notes are referred to as "pickup" notes. Even if the other instruments do not play anything before the first beat, a drummer will sometimes be asked to play pickup notes, which can also be called a "lead-in." The idea is to help all of the other instruments come in together on beat one of the first measure with a very clear idea of the tempo.

If everyone is going to start together on beat one, someone in the band will usually count off "1, 2, 3, 4" and everyone comes in at the same time. In many bands, the drummer sets the tempo by clicking his or her sticks together four times, just as the audio tracks in *The Drumset Musician* begin with four cowbell notes. But when playing pickups or lead-ins, you start during the initial count-off. If you are giving the band the tempo by clicking your sticks, you might only click them two or three times (giving them the first two or three quarter notes) before going into your lead-in. Once the band knows the tune well enough, you might be able to start the song by just playing the lead-in without having to count or click sticks at all.

### "Here and There"

**25** Audio track 25 is a ballad in verse/chorus form, with a four-bar intro. Before the first measure, the drums play a lead-in that begins one 16th before beat four. On the recording, you will hear three cowbell notes before the drums come in. The verses are played with a 16th feel on the hi-hat, with the snare drum playing cross-stick backbeats. The choruses maintain the 16th notes on the hi-hats, while the snare drum goes to regular backbeats on the drumhead and the bass drum goes to a two-bar pattern, the second bar of which is the same pattern that is played throughout the verses. Page 66 contains a chart with the exact drum part played on track 25.

## "Big Foot"

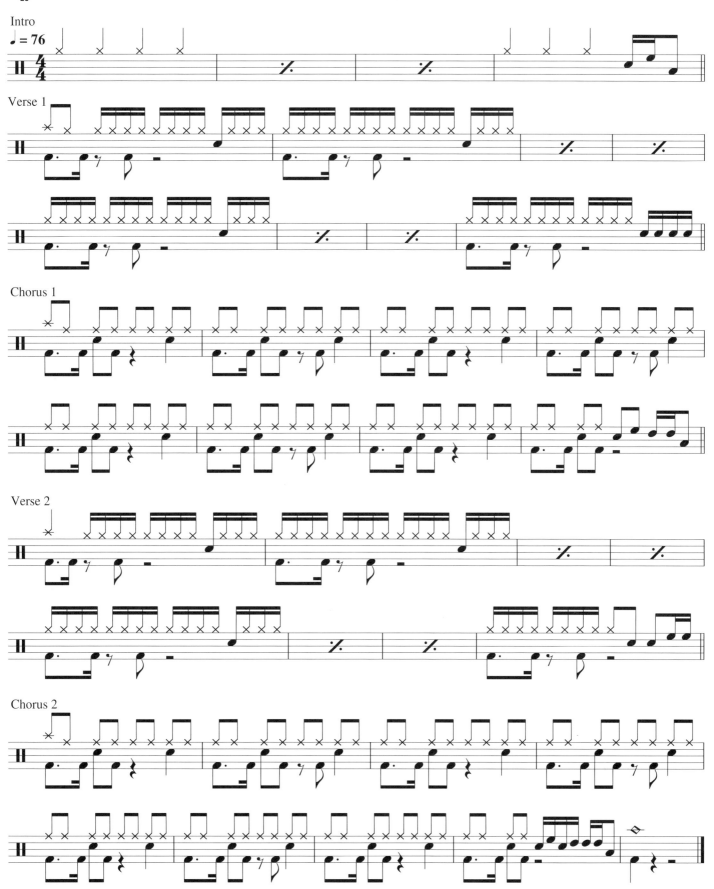

Track 24 is the same as track 23, except without drums. A cowbell maintains the quarter-note pulse, and a very soft shaker keeps the 16th-feel as a guide. First, learn to play the track with the "Big Foot" drum part from track 23, but then create your own drum part using different beats and fills from both Chapter Two and Chapter One.

## "Here and There"

Track 26 is the same as track 25, except without drums. A cowbell keeps the quarter-note pulse, a soft shaker plays 16ths, a tambourine plays backbeats, and a conga drum plays a 16th-based pattern. You can play along with this track using the "Here and There" chart from track 25, but then feel free to create your own drum part using various beats and fills from Chapters One and Two.

## "Slinky"

This song includes lots of syncopated grooving in the A-section bass drum and the B-section snare drum, along with upbeat hits in the last measure. Note: Although the first measure is in 6/4, the rest of the song is in 4/4, and so that is why there is a four-beat cowbell count-off.

Track 28 is the same as track 27 but without drums. You can play along with this track using the chart from track 27, but then feel free to create your own drum part using various beats and fills from Chapter Two and Chapter One.

# CHAPTER THREE
## Triplets and Shuffles

In Chapter One, we divided quarter notes in half (8th notes), and in Chapter Two we divided quarter notes into four parts (16th notes). Now we are going to divide quarter notes into thirds, which are called triplets. There is no note value in between an 8th note and a 16th note, so when the quarter note is being divided into thirds, 8th notes are used with a number 3 written over the top. This indicates that three triplet 8th notes are to be played in the time space that two "regular" 8th notes would normally occupy.

In 4/4 time, 8th-note triplets are notated and counted as in the example at right. Count "1 & a" etc. evenly; don't leave a space where the "e" would be if you were counting 16ths ("1 e & a" etc.).

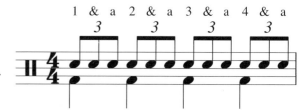

A popular rhythm, called the shuffle, consists of the first and third note of each triplet. Shuffles are played a lot in the blues style, as well as in rock 'n' roll and country music. The basic rhythm is notated at right.

## 12/8 Time

When triplets are mixed in with regular 8ths and 16ths, everything is usually notated in 4/4 time. But when all of the music is based around triplets, the same music can be notated in 12/8 time. What were triplets in 4/4 become straight 8ths in 12/8, and so they don't need number 3's over each group. What changes, though, is the 4/4 quarter-note pulse; in 12/8 time, the pulse becomes dotted-quarters in order to equal three 8th notes instead of two. To the right are examples of the straight 12/8 feel and the shuffle feel. Note that they are still counted the same way as in the 4/4 examples. (Try counting the 8th notes "1-2-3-4-5-6-7-8-9-10-11-12" at a quick tempo and you'll see why!)

As with previous chapters, you can add left-foot hi-hat when riding on the ride cymbal. Try maintaining the dotted-quarter pulse, as in the first example to the right, or reinforcing the backbeats, as in the lower example.

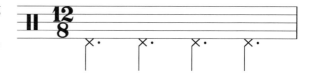

Listen to track 29 to hear how selected patterns from this chapter should sound. Once you are comfortable with the patterns on a page, try playing them along with tracks 31 and 33.

# Chapter Three Recorded Examples

**29** Audio track 29 features several examples from Chapter Three to give you an overview of the types of patterns you will be learning. For convenience, each of the patterns played on the track is notated below.

Backbeat Pattern 4a (page 70)

Backbeat Pattern 5b (page 70)

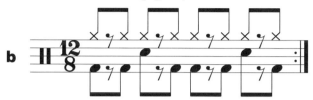

Backbeat Pattern 26a (page 73)

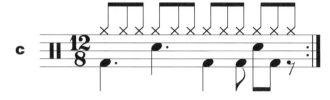

Half-time Feel 6b (page 74)

Snare Drum Variation 6b (page 75)

Dotted-quarter-note Ride Pattern 5 (page 76)

Shuffle Variations 1 (page 77)

Ride Variation 3 (page 78)

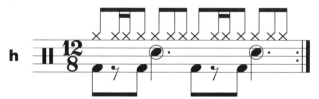

Tom-tom Beat 4 (page 78)

Drumset Colors 3 (page 78)

# Backbeat Patterns

The following four pages feature a variety of bass drum patterns with snare drum backbeats. The "a" patterns are built on straight 8th notes in 12/8, which is the same as a triplet feel in 4/4. The "b" patterns are based on the shuffle rhythm. Each corresponding "a" and "b" bass/snare pattern is played the same way, but in many cases, they are written differently to familiarize you with different styles of notation. You can play all the ride notes the same volume or accent the dotted-quarter pulse.

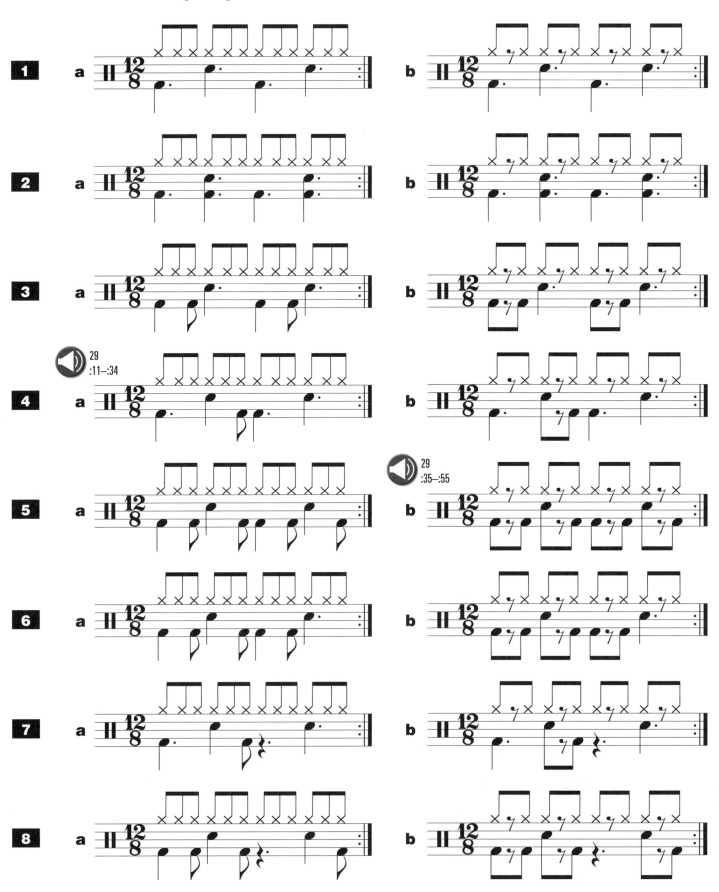

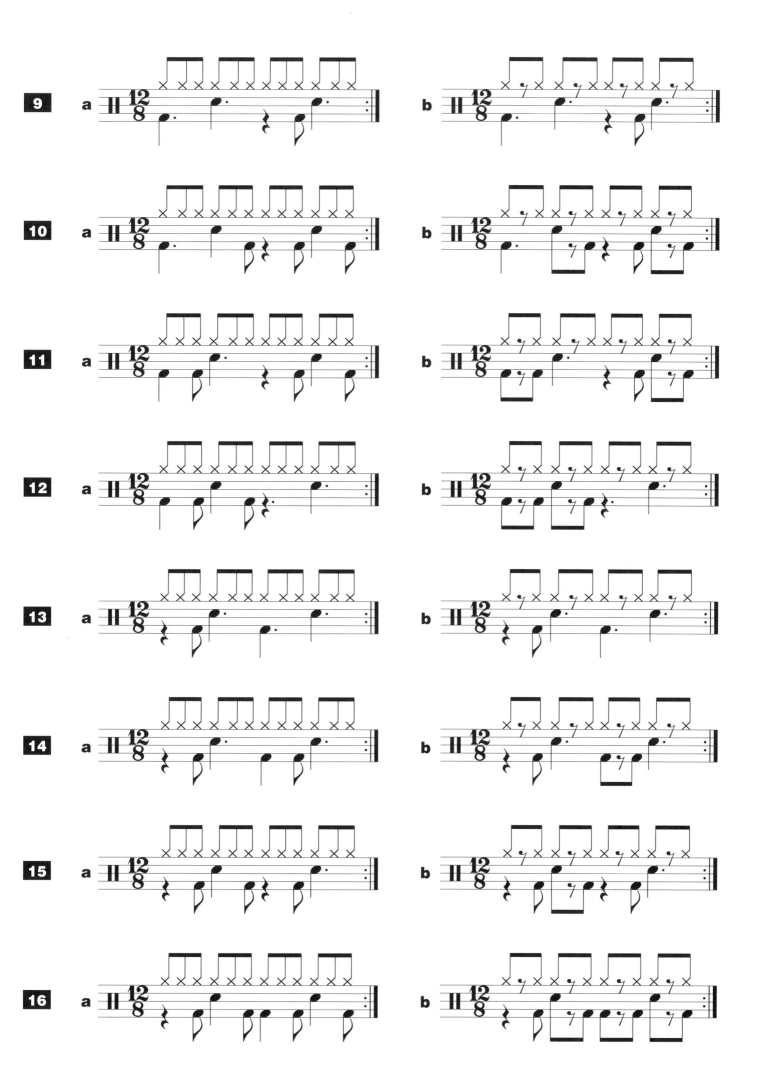

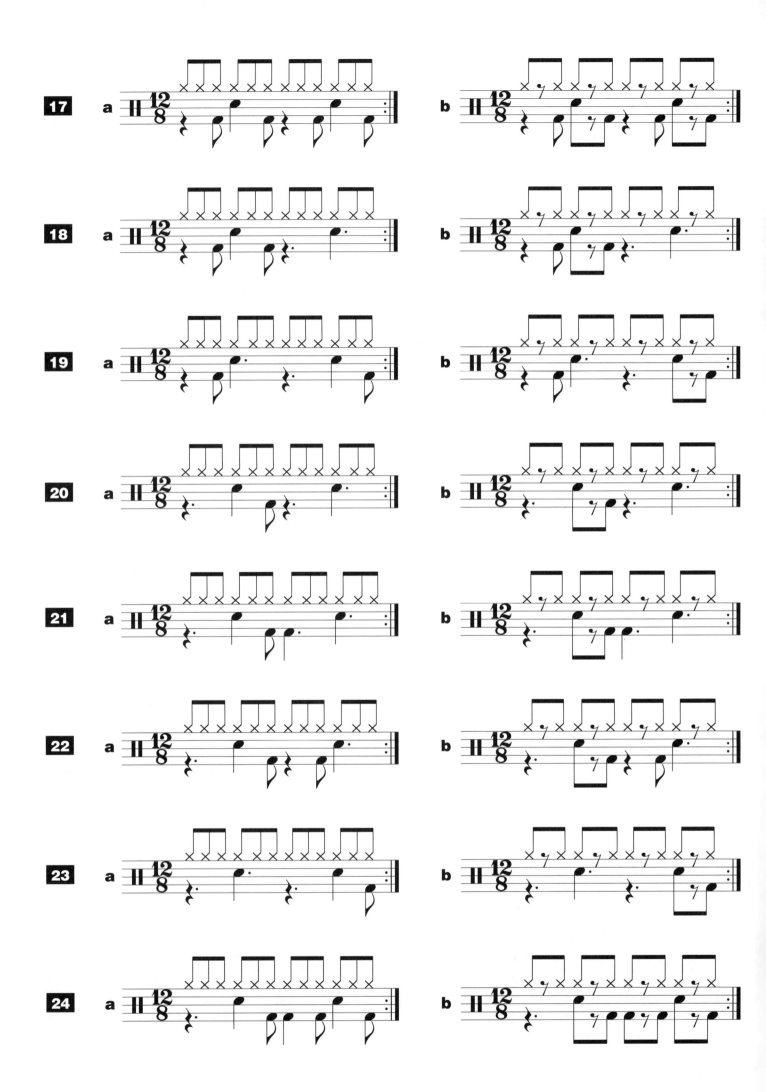

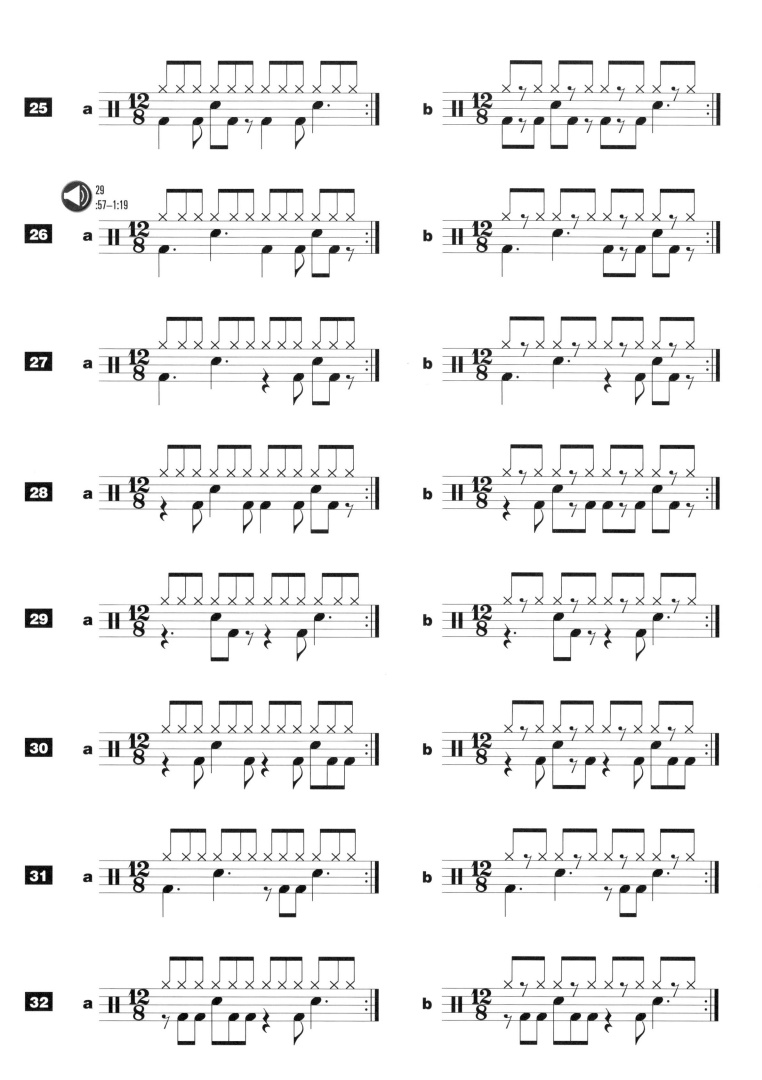

# Half-time Feel

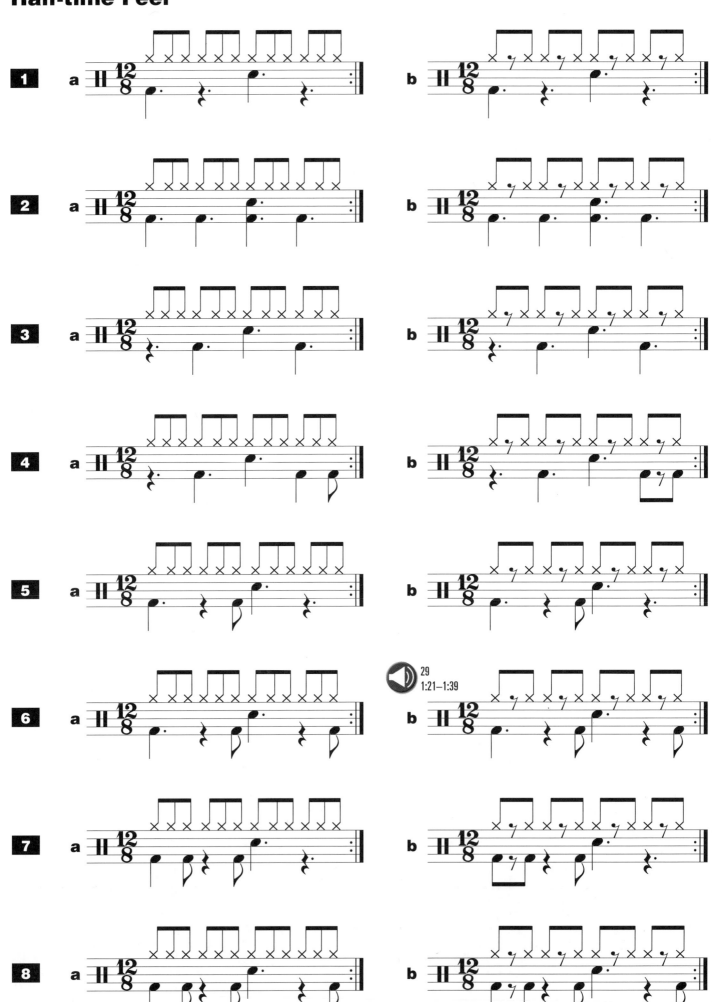

# Snare Drum Variations

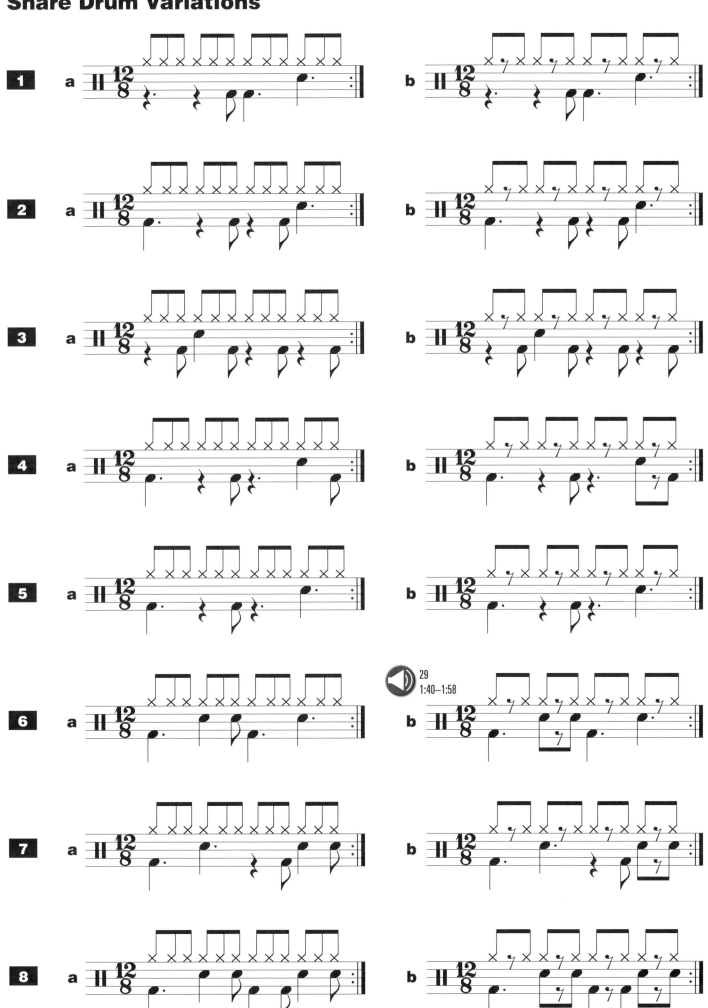

## Dotted-quarter-note Ride Patterns

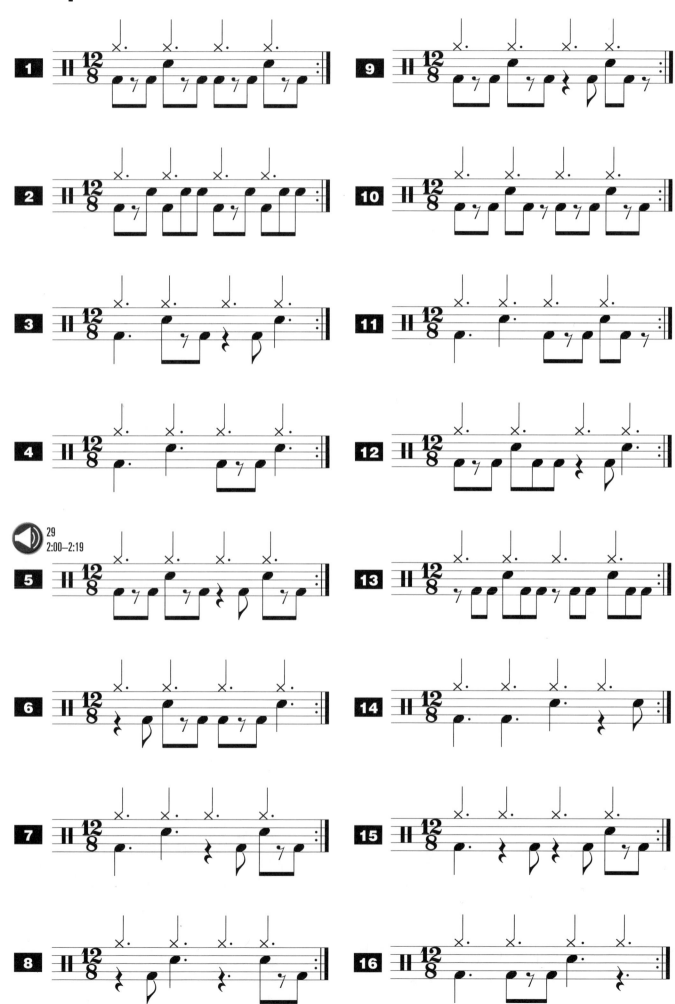

# Shuffle Variations

There are a variety of ways to play shuffles, as you will see from the examples below. Patterns 3 and 4 are especially useful for fast tempos, and patterns 4, 5, and 6 work well with either sticks or brushes.

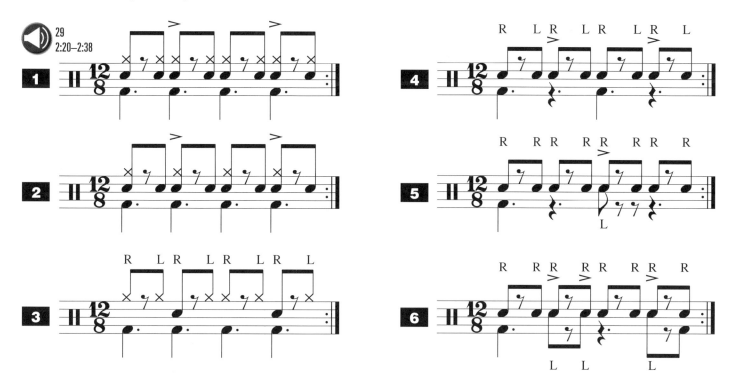

# Double Bass Beats

Many of the bass drum rhythms in this chapter can be applied to double bass drums or a double-bass pedal. In addition, drummers who have two bass drums or a double pedal often maintain continuous 8th notes with their feet, as in patterns 1 through 6 below, or keep a shuffle rhythm going with their feet as in patterns 7 and 8.

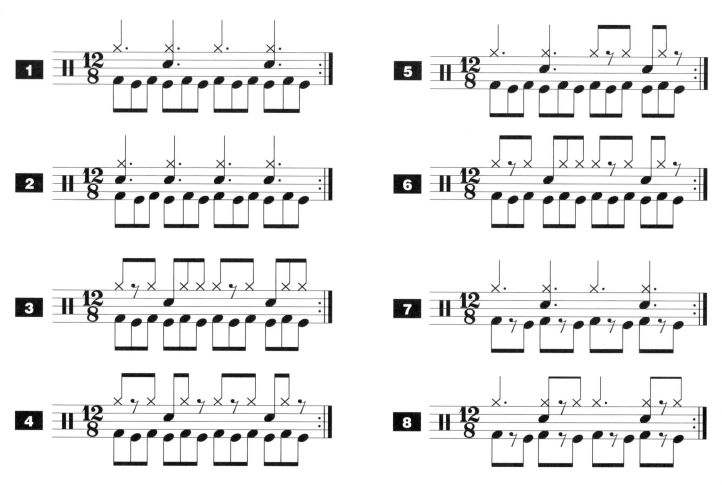

# Ride Variation

The ride pattern in examples 1 to 3 is especially useful for slow tempos.

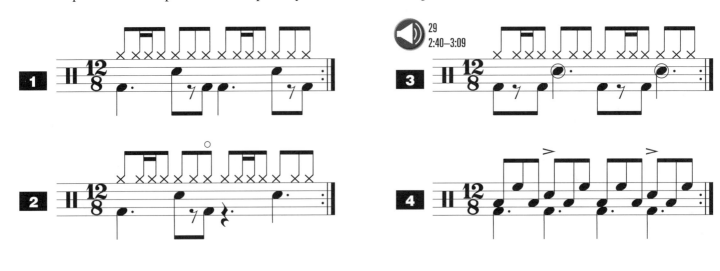

# Tom-tom Beats

Riding on the floor tom, as illustrated in pattern 4 below, can be applied to many of the patterns in this chapter.

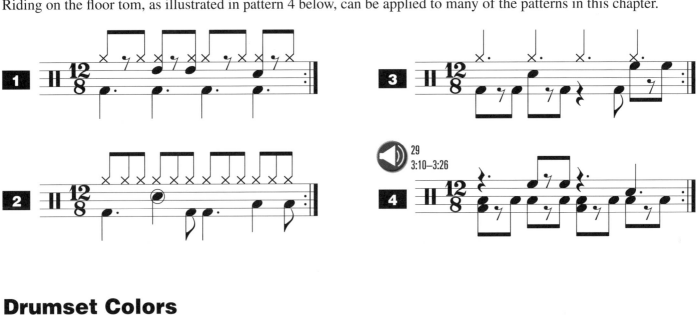

# Drumset Colors

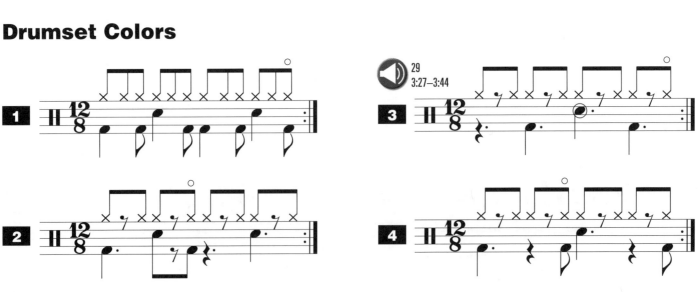

# Two-bar Patterns

# 12/8 Fills

Practice the basic fills on this page and the next with both the straight 12/8 feel and the shuffle feel, as illustrated in the charts at the top of the page. Feel free to substitute different snare and bass beats for the ones notated in the charts.

## 4-beat Fills

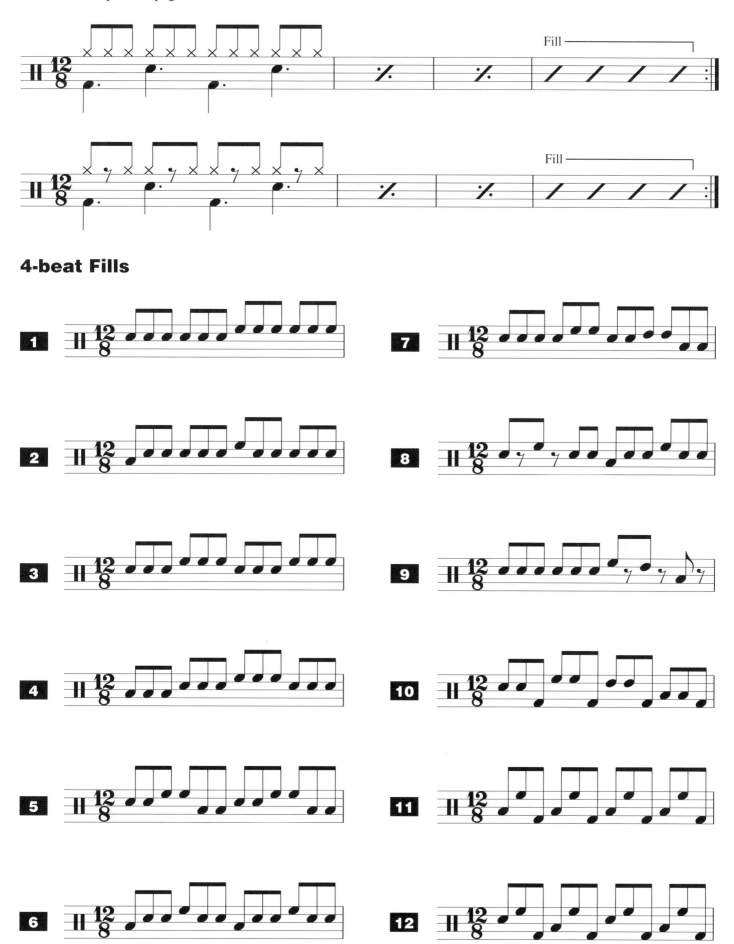

## 3-beat Fills

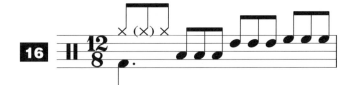

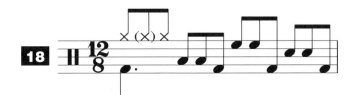

## 2-beat Fills

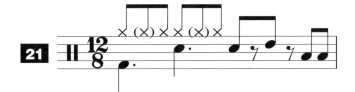

## 1-beat Fills

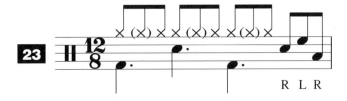

## Slow Blues

30  Audio track 30 consists of a slow 12-bar blues in which the following drum part is played.

 Track 31 is the same as track 30, except without drums. A cowbell maintains the dotted-quarter pulse while a shaker plays straight triplets. Play along with the track using the same beat used on track 30, but then try a variety of patterns from Chapter Three, as many of them will work fine.

31

 ## Medium Shuffle

32  Track 32 is a 12-bar blues with a medium shuffle feel, played three times through. The first time, the shuffle ride pattern is played on a tightly closed hi-hat; the second time, it is played on a slightly open hi-hat; the last time, the shuffle feel is played on ride cymbal. The bass and snare play a two-measure pattern. Fills are played at the end of each 12 bars. Use the following chart as a guide to the drum part on the recording.

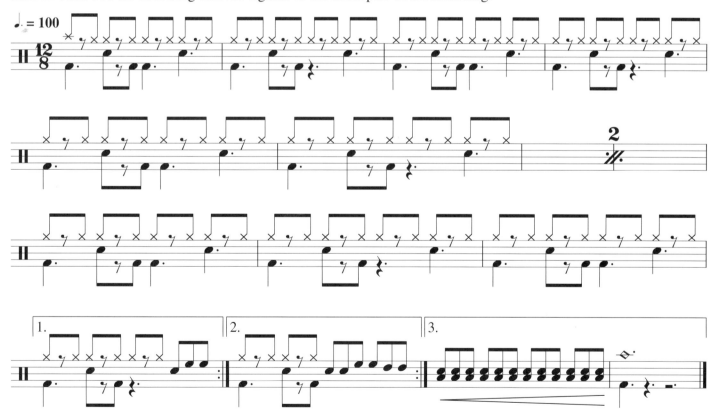

 Track 33 is the same as track 32, but without drums. Play along with it using the above chart, but then feel free to play along using other shuffle patterns from throughout Chapter Three.

33

# Musical Form, Part Three

## Endings

Just as some songs have some extra measures at the beginning, called an intro, songs can also have extra bars at the end, which can be known as an "outro" (opposite of "intro"), a "coda," or a "tag." In many cases, the drums play the same pattern used elsewhere in the song. But as with intros, during the ending the drummer might play a simplified version of whatever was played in the song, to help indicate that the tune is coming to an end.

### "Country Living"

34    Audio track 34 contains a slow country ballad in the verse/chorus form. Although previous tracks in this style have featured songs in which the verses and choruses each contain the same number of measures, either can be longer or shorter than the other. In "Country Living" the verses are each eight measures and the choruses are four measures. The song also contains a two-measure intro with a one-beat lead-in on the drums, as well as an "outro" that uses the same pattern as the intro and verses.

The chart on the next page shows the complete drum part that is played on track 34. To distinguish between the verses and choruses, the ride pattern is different in each, and it switches from hi-hat to ride cymbal. Also, the snare drum plays cross-stick backbeats during the verses and regular hits during the choruses. Note how fills are used to signal that one section is ending and another is about to begin.

35    Track 35 is the same as track 34 except without drums. As a guide, a cowbell maintains the dotted-quarter pulse, a click sound fills in the 8th notes, and a tambourine plays backbeats. Play along with the track using the chart from track 34, and then create your own drum part using patterns and ideas from throughout Chapter Three.

## The Bridge

Besides verses, choruses, intros, and endings, many songs have a section called a bridge. Generally, the bridge is played only once and is different than the verses and choruses. It might have a different melody, different harmony (chords), different lyrics, and/or a different beat or feel. In some songs that have vocals, the bridge might be the section in which guitar, keyboard, or other solos are played.

### "Down 'n' Dirty"

36    Not every blues-style song is written in a 12-bar format, as illustrated by "Down 'n' Dirty," heard with drums on track 36. The song is in verse/chorus form, and it has an intro and a bridge. Notice that verses and choruses do not always have to alternate; after the intro, two verses are played before the first chorus, and the song ends with two choruses.

The drum part on the intro simply consists of backbeats played on a slightly open hi-hat. The drum part in the verses emphasizes offbeats in the bass drum, which accent the rhythm played by the rhythm guitar and bass. The drum part in the chorus is more straight ahead, with the dotted-quarter ride pattern switching to cymbal. The drum part on the bridge is in strong contrast to the verse and chorus sections. A shuffle is played on the hi-hat, with snare drum striking on beat three of each bar, creating a half-time feel. Notice how fills and cymbal crashes are used to signal the beginnings and ends of different sections. A chart of the complete drum part to "Down 'n' Dirty" appears on page 86.

37    Track 37 is the same as track 36, except without drums. A cowbell maintains the dotted-quarter pulse, while a tambourine plays straight backbeats during the verses and choruses, and a half-time backbeat (on beat three) during the bridge. Play along with the track using the chart on page 86, and then create your own part using different patterns and fills from Chapter Three.

## "Country Living"

## "Down 'n' Dirty"

**"M80"**

This song features a groove in which the right hand plays floor tom and the left hand plays small tom, except for the backbeats, which are on snare drum. The B sections contrast the tom-tom-based A sections with a one-measure shuffle groove. Note the double crashes that happen in two places during the B sections.

Track 39 is the same as track 38, except without drums. Play along with the track using the chart from track 38, and then create your own drum part using patterns and ideas from throughout Chapter Three.

# Conclusion

The various patterns in this book only scratch the surface of what is possible with drumming. But always remember that the drummer's first job is to make the music feel good, and a simple pattern played well is more impressive than a complex pattern played badly. When creating drum parts, always pay attention to the form of the music so that you are truly playing the song and not just playing a bunch of beats and fills. Don't just be a drummer, be a drumset musician!

# YOU CAN'T BEAT OUR DRUM BOOKS!

### Learn to Play the Drumset – Book 1
*by Peter Magadini*
This unique method starts students out on the entire drumset and teaches them the basics in the shortest amount of time. Book 1 covers basic 4- and 5-piece set-ups, grips and sticks, reading and improvisation, coordination of hands and feet, and features a variety of contemporary and basic rhythm patterns with exercise breakdowns for each.
06620030  Book/CD Pack.................................................. $14.99

### Creative Timekeeping for the Contemporary Jazz Drummer
*by Rick Mattingly*
Combining a variety of jazz ride cymbal patterns with coordination and reading exercises, *Creative Timekeeping* develops true independence: the ability to play any rhythm on the ride cymbal while playing any rhythm on the snare and bass drums. It provides a variety of jazz ride cymbal patterns as well as coordination and reading exercises that can be played along with them. Five chapters: Ride Cymbal Patterns; Coordination Patterns and Reading; Combination Patterns and Reading; Applications; and Cymbal Reading.
06621764 ........................................................................ $9.99

### The Drumset Musician – 2nd Edition
*by Rod Morgenstein and Rick Mattingly*
Containing hundreds of practical, usable beats and fills, The Drumset Musician teaches you how to apply a variety of patterns and grooves to the actual performance of songs. The accompanying online audio includes demos as well as 18 play-along tracks covering a wide range of rock, blues and pop styles, with detailed instructions on how to create exciting, solid drum parts.
00268369  Book/Online Audio ......................................... $19.99

### Drum Aerobics
*by Andy Ziker*
A 52-week, one-exercise-per-day workout program for developing, improving, and maintaining drum technique. Players of all levels – beginners to advanced – will increase their speed, coordination, dexterity and accuracy. The online audio contains all 365 workout licks, plus play-along grooves in styles including rock, blues, jazz, heavy metal, reggae, funk, calypso, bossa nova, march, mambo, New Orleans 2nd Line, and lots more!
06620137  Book/Online Audio ......................................... $19.99

### 40 Intermediate Snare Drum Solos
For Concert Performance
*by Ben Hans*
This book provides the advancing percussionist with interesting solo material in all musical styles. It is designed as a lesson supplement, or as performance material for recitals and solo competitions. Includes: 40 intermediate snare drum solos presented in easy-to-read notation; a music glossary; Percussive Arts Society rudiment chart; suggested sticking, dynamics and articulation markings; and much more!
06620067 ........................................................................ $8.99

### Joe Porcaro's Drumset Method – Groovin' with Rudiments
Patterns Applied to Rock, Jazz & Latin Drumset
*by Joe Porcaro*
Master teacher Joe Porcaro presents rudiments at the drumset this sensational new edition of *Groovin' with Rudiments*. T book is chock full of exciting drum grooves, sticking patterns, fi polyrhythmic adaptations, odd meters, and fantastic solo ideas jazz, rock, and Latin feels. The online audio features 99 audio examples in many styles to round out this true collection of sup drumming material for every serious drumset performer.
06620129  Book/Online Audio ........................................ $24

### Show Drumming
The Essential Guide to Playing Drumset for Live Shows and Musicals
*by Ed Shaughnessy and Clem DeRosa*
Who better to teach you than "America's Premier Showdrumm himself, Mr. Ed Shaughnessy! Features: a step-by-step walk-thro of a simulated show; CD with music, comments & tips from notated examples; practical tips; advice on instruments; a spe accessories section with photos; and more!
06620080  Book/CD Pack.................................................. $16.

### Instant Guide to Drum Grooves
The Essential Reference for the Working Drummer
*by Maria Martinez*
Become a more versatile drumset player! From traditional Dixiela to cutting-edge hip-hop, Instant Guide to Drum Grooves is a ha source featuring 100 patterns that will prepare working drumm for the stylistic variety of modern gigs. The book includes essen beats and grooves in such styles as: jazz, shuffle, country, ro funk, New Orleans, reggae, calypso, Brazilian and Latin.
06620056  Book/CD Pack.................................................. $10.

### The Complete Drumset Rudiments
*by Peter Magadini*
Use your imagination to incorporate these rudimental etudes i new patterns that you can apply to the drumset or tom toms you develop your hand technique with the Snare Drum Rudime your hand and foot technique with the Drumset Rudiments a your polyrhythmic technique with the Polyrhythm Rudime Adopt them all into your own creative expressions based on id you come up with while practicing.
06620016  Book/CD Pack.................................................. $14

### Drum Dictionary
An A-Z Guide to Tips, Techniques & Much More
*by Ed Roscetti*
Take your playing from ordinary to extraordinary in this encompassing book/audio package for drummers. Yo receive valuable tips on performing, recording, the music busine instruments and equipment, beats, fills, soloing techniques, c and maintenance, and more. Styles such as rock, jazz, hip-h and Latin are represented through demonstrations of authe grooves and instruments appropriate for each genre.
00244646  Book/Online Audio ........................................ $19

Prices, contents, and availability subject to change without notice.

**HAL•LEONARD®**

www.halleonard.com

0